McDougal Littell Science

Electricity
and
Magnetism

magnet

ATTRACT

magnetic field

PHYSICAL SCIENCE

A ▶ Matter and Energy
B ▶ Chemical Interactions
C ▶ Motion and Forces
D ▶ Waves, Sound, and Light
E ▶ Electricity and Magnetism

LIFE SCIENCE

A ▶ Cells and Heredity
B ▶ Life Over Time
C ▶ Diversity of Living Things
D ▶ Ecology
E ▶ Human Biology

EARTH SCIENCE

A ▶ Earth's Surface
B ▶ The Changing Earth
C ▶ Earth's Waters
D ▶ Earth's Atmosphere
E ▶ Space Science

Acknowledgments: Excerpts and adaptations from *National Science Education Standards* by the National Academy of Sciences. Copyright © 1996 by the National Academy of Sciences. Reprinted with permission from the National Academies Press, Washington, D.C.

Excerpts and adaptations from *Benchmarks for Science Literacy: Project 2061.* Copyright © 1993 by the American Association for the Advancement of Science. Reprinted with permission.

Printed in the United States of America.

ISBN-13: 978-0-618-84257-5

ISBN-10: 0-618-84257-8

7 8   2266   16

4500581209

Internet Web Site: http://www.mcdougallittell.com

Science Consultants

Chief Science Consultant

James Trefil, Ph.D. is the Clarence J. Robinson Professor of Physics at George Mason University. He is the author or co-author of more than 25 books, including *Science Matters* and *The Nature of Science*. Dr. Trefil is a member of the American Association for the Advancement of Science's Committee on the Public Understanding of Science and Technology. He is also a fellow of the World Economic Forum and a frequent contributor to *Smithsonian* magazine.

Rita Ann Calvo, Ph.D. is Senior Lecturer in Molecular Biology and Genetics at Cornell University, where for 12 years she also directed the Cornell Institute for Biology Teachers. Dr. Calvo is the 1999 recipient of the College and University Teaching Award from the National Association of Biology Teachers.

Kenneth Cutler, M.S. is the Education Coordinator for the Julius L. Chambers Biomedical Biotechnology Research Institute at North Carolina Central University. A former middle school and high school science teacher, he received a 1999 Presidential Award for Excellence in Science Teaching.

Instructional Design Consultants

Douglas Carnine, Ph.D. is Professor of Education and Director of the National Center for Improving the Tools of Educators at the University of Oregon. He is the author of seven books and over 100 other scholarly publications, primarily in the areas of instructional design and effective instructional strategies and tools for diverse learners. Dr. Carnine also serves as a member of the National Institute for Literacy Advisory Board.

Linda Carnine, Ph.D. consults with school districts on curriculum development and effective instruction for students struggling academically. A former teacher and school administrator, Dr. Carnine also co-authored a popular remedial reading program.

Donald Steely, Ph.D. serves as principal investigator at the Oregon Center for Applied Science (ORCAS) on federal grants for science and language arts programs. His background also includes teaching and authoring of print and multimedia programs in science, mathematics, history, and spelling.

Sam Miller, Ph.D. is a middle school science teacher and the Teacher Development Liaison for the Eugene, Oregon, Public Schools. He is the author of curricula for teaching science, mathematics, computer skills, and language arts.

Vicky Vachon, Ph.D. consults with school districts throughout the United States and Canada on improving overall academic achievement with a focus on literacy. She is also co-author of a widely used program for remedial readers.

Content Reviewers

John Beaver, Ph.D.
Ecology
Professor, Director of Science Education Center
College of Education and Human Services
Western Illinois University
Macomb, IL

Donald J. DeCoste, Ph.D.
Matter and Energy, Chemical Interactions
Chemistry Instructor
University of Illinois
Urbana-Champaign, IL

Dorothy Ann Fallows, Ph.D., MSc
Diversity of Living Things, Microbiology
Partners in Health
Boston, MA

Michael Foote, Ph.D.
The Changing Earth, Life Over Time
Associate Professor
Department of the Geophysical Sciences
The University of Chicago
Chicago, IL

Lucy Fortson, Ph.D.
Space Science
Director of Astronomy
Adler Planetarium and Astronomy Museum
Chicago, IL

Elizabeth Godrick, Ph.D.
Human Biology
Professor, CAS Biology
Boston University
Boston, MA

Isabelle Sacramento Grilo, M.S.
The Changing Earth
Lecturer, Department of the Geological Sciences
San Diego State University
San Diego, CA

David Harbster, MSc
Diversity of Living Things
Professor of Biology
Paradise Valley Community College
Phoenix, AZ

Richard D. Norris, Ph.D.
Earth's Waters
Professor of Paleobiology
Scripps Institution of Oceanography
University of California, San Diego
La Jolla, CA

Donald B. Peck, M.S.
*Motion and Forces; Waves, Sound, and Light;
 Electricity and Magnetism*
Director of the Center for Science Education (retired)
Fairleigh Dickinson University
Madison, NJ

Javier Penalosa, Ph.D.
Diversity of Living Things, Plants
Associate Professor, Biology Department
Buffalo State College
Buffalo, NY

Raymond T. Pierrehumbert, Ph.D.
Earth's Atmosphere
Professor in Geophysical Sciences (Atmospheric Science)
The University of Chicago
Chicago, IL

Brian J. Skinner, Ph.D.
Earth's Surface
Eugene Higgins Professor of Geology and Geophysics
Yale University
New Haven, CT

Nancy E. Spaulding, M.S.
Earth's Surface, The Changing Earth, Earth's Waters
Earth Science Teacher (retired)
Elmira Free Academy
Elmira, NY

Steven S. Zumdahl, Ph.D.
Matter and Energy, Chemical Interactions
Professor Emeritus of Chemistry
University of Illinois
Urbana-Champaign, IL

Susan L. Zumdahl, M.S.
Matter and Energy, Chemical Interactions
Chemistry Education Specialist
University of Illinois
Urbana-Champaign, IL

Safety Consultant

Juliana Texley, Ph.D.
Former K–12 Science Teacher and School Superintendent
Boca Raton, FL

English Language Advisor

Judy Lewis, M.A.
Director, State and Federal Programs for reading proficiency
and high risk populations
Rancho Cordova, CA

Teacher Panel Members

Carol Arbour
Tallmadge Middle School,
Tallmadge, OH

Patty Belcher
Goodrich Middle School,
Akron, OH

Gwen Broestl
Luis Munoz Marin Middle School,
Cleveland, OH

Al Brofman
Tehipite Middle School,
Fresno, CA

John Cockrell
Clinton Middle School,
Columbus, OH

Jenifer Cox
Sylvan Middle School,
Citrus Heights, CA

Linda Culpepper
Martin Middle School,
Charlotte, NC

Kathleen Ann DeMatteo
Margate Middle School,
Margate, FL

Melvin Figueroa
New River Middle School,
Ft. Lauderdale, FL

Doretha Grier
Kannapolis Middle School,
Kannapolis, NC

Robert Hood
Alexander Hamilton Middle School,
Cleveland, OH

Scott Hudson
Covedale Elementary School,
Cincinnati, OH

Loretta Langdon
Princeton Middle School,
Princeton, NC

Carlyn Little
Glades Middle School,
Miami, FL

Ann Marie Lynn
Amelia Earhart Middle School,
Riverside, CA

James Minogue
Lowe's Grove Middle School,
Durham, NC

Joann Myers
Buchanan Middle School,
Tampa, FL

Barbara Newell
Charles Evans Hughes Middle School,
Long Beach, CA

Anita Parker
Kannapolis Middle School,
Kannapolis, NC

Greg Pirolo
Golden Valley Middle School,
San Bernardino, CA

Laura Pottmyer
Apex Middle School,
Apex, NC

Lynn Prichard
Booker T. Washington Middle Magnet
School, Tampa, FL

Jacque Quick
Walter Williams High School,
Burlington, NC

Robert Glenn Reynolds
Hillman Middle School,
Youngstown, OH

Stacy Rinehart
Lufkin Road Middle School,
Apex, NC

Theresa Short
Abbott Middle School,
Fayetteville, NC

Rita Slivka
Alexander Hamilton Middle School,
Cleveland, OH

Marie Sofsak
B F Stanton Middle School,
Alliance, OH

Nancy Stubbs
Sweetwater Union Unified School District,
Chula Vista, CA

Sharon Stull
Quail Hollow Middle School,
Charlotte, NC

Donna Taylor
Okeeheelee Middle School,
West Palm Beach, FL

Sandi Thompson
Harding Middle School,
Lakewood, OH

Lori Walker
Audubon Middle School & Magnet Center,
Los Angeles, CA

Teacher Lab Evaluators

Andrew Boy
W.E.B. DuBois Academy,
Cincinnati, OH

Jill Brimm-Byrne
Albany Park Academy,
Chicago, IL

Gwen Broestl
Luis Munoz Marin Middle School,
Cleveland, OH

Al Brofman
Tehipite Middle School,
Fresno, CA

Michael A. Burstein
The Rashi School,
Newton, MA

Trudi Coutts
Madison Middle School,
Naperville, IL

Jenifer Cox
Sylvan Middle School,
Citrus Heights, CA

Larry Cwik
Madison Middle School,
Naperville, IL

Jennifer Donatelli
Kennedy Junior High School,
Lisle, IL

Melissa Dupree
Lakeside Middle School,
Evans, GA

Carl Fechko
Luis Munoz Marin Middle School,
Cleveland, OH

Paige Fullhart
Highland Middle School,
Libertyville, IL

Sue Hood
Glen Crest Middle School,
Glen Ellyn, IL

William Luzader
Plymouth Community Intermediate School,
Plymouth, MA

Ann Min
Beardsley Middle School,
Crystal Lake, IL

Aileen Mueller
Kennedy Junior High School,
Lisle, IL

Nancy Nega
Churchville Middle School,
Elmhurst, IL

Oscar Newman
Sumner Math and Science Academy,
Chicago, IL

Lynn Prichard
Booker T. Washington Middle Magnet
School, Tampa, FL

Jacque Quick
Walter Williams High School,
Burlington, NC

Stacy Rinehart
Lufkin Road Middle School,
Apex, NC

Seth Robey
Gwendolyn Brooks Middle School,
Oak Park, IL

Kevin Steele
Grissom Middle School,
Tinley Park, IL

Electricity and Magnetism

Unit Features

1 Electricity   6

(the **BIG** idea)

Moving electric charges transfer energy.

2 Circuits and Electronics   40

(the **BIG** idea)

Circuits control the flow of electric charge.

How can circuits control the flow of charge? page 40

What force is acting on this compass needle?
page 76

3 Magnetism 76

Features

Visual Highlights

Internet Resources @ ClassZone.com

INVESTIGATIONS AND ACTIVITIES

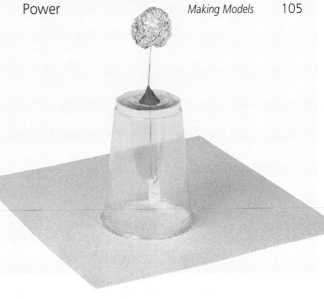

Standards and Benchmarks

Each chapter in **Electricity and Magnetism** covers some of the learning goals that are described in the *National Science Education Standards* (NSES) and the Project 2061 *Benchmarks for Science Literacy*. Selected content and skill standards are shown below in shortened form. The following National Science Education Standards are covered on pages xii–xxvii, in Frontiers in Science, and in Timelines in Science, as well as in chapter features and laboratory investigations: Understandings About Scientific Inquiry (A.9), Understandings About Science and Technology (E.6), Science and Technology in Society (F.5), Science as a Human Endeavor (G.1), Nature of Science (G.2), and History of Science (G.3).

Content Standards

1 Electricity

National Science Education Standards

B.3.a	Energy • is often associated with electricity • is transferred in many ways
B.3.e	In most chemical reactions, energy is transferred into or out of the system. Heat, light, motion, or electricity might be involved in this transfer.

Project 2061 Benchmarks

3.A.3	Engineers and others who work in design and technology use scientific knowledge to solve practical problems.

2 Circuits and Electronics

National Science Education Standards

B.3.a	Energy. is property of substances that is often associated with electricity. Energy is transferred in many ways.
B.3.d	Circuits transfer electrical energy. Heat, light, sound, and chemical changes are produced.

Project 2061 Benchmarks

1.C.6	Computers are important in science.
3.A.2	Technology is important in the computation and communication of information.
8.D.2	The ability to code information or electric currents in wires has made communication many times faster than is possible by mail or sound.
8.E.1	Computers use digital codes containing only two symbols to perform all operations. Analog signals must be converted into digital codes before a computer can process them.
9.A.6	Numbers can be represented by using only 1 and 0.

3 Magnetism

Project 2061 Benchmarks

4.G.3	Electric currents and magnets can exert a force on each other.
8.C.4	Electrical energy can be produced from a variety of energy sources and can be transformed into almost any other form of energy. Electricity is used to distribute energy quickly and conveniently to distant locations.

Process and Skill Standards

	National Science Education Standards		Project 2061 Benchmarks
A.1	Identify questions that can be answered through investigation.	1.A.3	Some knowledge in science is very old and yet is still used today.
A.2	Design and conduct a scientific investigation.	1.C.1	Contributions to science and technology have been made by different people, in different cultures, at different times.
A.3	Use appropriate tools and techniques to gather and interpret data.		
A.4	Use evidence to describe, predict, explain, and model.	3.B.1	Design requires taking constraints into account.
A.5	Use critical thinking to find relationships between results and interpretations.	3.B.2	Technologies have effects other than those intended.
A.6	Consider alternative explanations and predictions.	8.B.1	The choice of materials for a job depends on their properties.
A.7	Communicate procedures, results, and conclusions.	9.A.3	How decimals should be written depends on how precise the measurements are.
A.8	Use mathematics in scientific investigations.	9.A.7	Computations can give more digits than make sense or are useful.
E.1	Identify a problem to be reached.		
E.2	Design a solution or product.	9.B.3	Graphs can show the relationship between two variables.
E.3	Implement the proposed solution.	9.C.4	Graphs show patterns and can be used to make predictions.
E.4	Evaluate the solution or design.		
E.5	Communicate the process of technological design.	11.C.4	Use equations to summarize observed changes.
F.4.c	Use systematic thinking to eliminate risks.	12.B.1	Find what percentage one number is of another.
F.4.d	Decisions are made based on estimated risks and benefits.	12.B.8	Round a calculation to the correct number of significant figures.
		12.C.1	Compare amounts proportionally.
		12.C.5	Inspect, disassemble, and reassemble simple devices and describe what the various parts are for.
		12.D.1	Use tables and graphs to organize information and identify relationships.
		12.D.2	Read, interpret, and describe tables and graphs.
		12.D.4	Understand information that includes different types of charts and graphs, including circle charts, bar graphs, line graphs, data tables, diagrams, and symbols.
		12.E.3	Be skeptical of arguments based on samples for which there was no control group.
		12.E.4	There may be more than one good way to interpret scientific findings.

Introducing Physical Science

Scientists are curious. Since ancient times, they have been asking and answering questions about the world around them. Scientists are also very suspicious of the answers they get. They carefully collect evidence and test their answers many times before accepting an idea as correct.

In this book you will see how scientific knowledge keeps growing and changing as scientists ask new questions and rethink what was known before. The following sections will help get you started.

What Is Physical Science?

In the simplest terms, physical science is the study of what things are made of and how they change. It combines the studies of both physics and chemistry. Physics is the science of matter, energy, and forces. It includes the study of topics such as motion, light, and electricity and magnetism. Chemistry is the study of the structure and properties of matter, and it especially focuses on how substances change into different substances.

The text and pictures in this book will help you learn key concepts and important facts about physical science. A variety of activities will help you investigate these concepts. As you learn, it helps to have a big picture of physical science as a framework for this new information. The four unifying principles listed below will give you this big picture. Read the next few pages to get an overview of each of these principles and a sense of why they are so important.

- **Matter is made of particles too small to see.**

- **Matter changes form and moves from place to place.**

- **Energy changes from one form to another, but it cannot be created or destroyed.**

- **Physical forces affect the movement of all matter on Earth and throughout the universe.**

the **BIG** idea

Each chapter begins with a big idea. Keep in mind that each big idea relates to one or more of the unifying principles.

Matter is made of particles too small to see.

This simple statement is the basis for explaining an amazing variety of things about the world. For example, it explains why substances can exist as solids, liquids, and gases, and why wood burns but iron does not. Like the tiles that make up this mosaic picture, the particles that make up all substances combine to make patterns and structures that can be seen. Unlike these tiles, the individual particles themselves are far too small to see.

What It Means

To understand this principle better, let's take a closer look at the two key words: *matter* and *particles.*

Matter

Objects you can see and touch are all around you. The materials that these objects are made of are called **matter.** All living things—even you—are also matter. Even though you can't see it, the air around you is matter too. Scientists often say that matter is anything that has mass and takes up space. **Mass** is a measure of the amount of matter in an object. We use the word **volume** to refer to the amount of space an object or a substance takes up.

Particles

The tiny particles that make up all matter are called **atoms.** Just how tiny are atoms? They are far too small to see, even through a powerful microscope. In fact, an atom is more than a million times smaller than the period at the end of this sentence.

There are more than 100 basic kinds of matter called **elements.** For example, iron, gold, and oxygen are three common elements. Each element has its own unique kind of atom. The atoms of any element are all alike but different from the atoms of any other element.

Many familiar materials are made of particles called molecules. In a **molecule,** two or more atoms stick together to form a larger particle. For example, a water molecule is made of two atoms of hydrogen and one atom of oxygen.

Why It's Important

Understanding atoms and molecules makes it possible to explain and predict the behavior of matter. Among other things, this knowledge allows scientists to

- explain why different materials have different characteristics
- predict how a material will change when heated or cooled
- figure out how to combine atoms and molecules to make new and useful materials

Matter changes form and moves from place to place.

You see matter change form every day. You see the ice in your glass of juice disappear without a trace. You see a black metal gate slowly develop a flaky, orange coating. Matter is constantly changing and moving.

What It Means

Remember that matter is made of tiny particles called atoms. Atoms are constantly moving and combining with one another. All changes in matter are the result of atoms moving and combining in different ways.

Matter Changes and Moves

You can look at water to see how matter changes and moves. A block of ice is hard like a rock. Leave the ice out in sunlight, however, and it changes into a puddle of water. That puddle of water can eventually change into water vapor and disappear into the air. The water vapor in the air can become raindrops, which may fall on rocks, causing them to weather and wear away. The water that flows in rivers and streams picks up tiny bits of rock and carries them from one shore to another. Understanding how the world works requires an understanding of how matter changes and moves.

Matter Is Conserved

No matter was lost in any of the changes described above. The ice turned to water because its molecules began to move more quickly as they got warmer. The bits of rock carried away by the flowing river were not gone forever. They simply ended up farther down the river. The puddles of rainwater didn't really disappear; their molecules slowly mixed with molecules in the air.

Under ordinary conditions, when matter changes form, no matter is created or destroyed. The water created by melting ice has the same mass as the ice did. If you could measure the water vapor that mixes with the air, you would find it had the same mass as the water in the puddle did.

Why It's Important

Understanding how mass is conserved when matter changes form has helped scientists to

- describe changes they see in the world
- predict what will happen when two substances are mixed
- explain where matter goes when it seems to disappear

Energy changes from one form to another, but it cannot be created or destroyed.

When you use energy to warm your food or to turn on a flashlight, you may think that you "use up" the energy. Even though the camp-stove fuel is gone and the flashlight battery no longer functions, the energy they provided has not disappeared. It has been changed into a form you can no longer use. Understanding how energy changes forms is the basis for understanding how heat, light, and motion are produced.

What It Means

Changes that you see around you depend on energy. **Energy,** in fact, means the ability to cause change. The electrical energy from an outlet changes into light and heat in a light bulb. Plants change the light energy from the Sun into chemical energy, which animals use to power their muscles.

Energy Changes Forms

Using energy means changing energy. You probably have seen electric energy changing into light, heat, sound, and mechanical energy in household appliances. Fuels like wood, coal, and oil contain chemical energy that produces heat when burned. Electric power plants make electrical energy from a variety of energy sources, including falling water, nuclear energy, and fossil fuels.

Energy Is Conserved

Energy can be converted into forms that can be used for specific purposes. During the conversion, some of the original energy is converted into unwanted forms. For instance, when a power plant converts the energy of falling water into electrical energy, some of the energy is lost to friction and sound.

Similarly, when electrical energy is used to run an appliance, some of the energy is converted into forms that are not useful. Only a small percentage of the energy used in a light bulb, for instance, produces light; most of the energy becomes heat. Nonetheless, the total amount of energy remains the same through all these conversions.

The fact that energy does not disappear is a law of physical science. The **law of conservation of energy** states that energy cannot be created or destroyed. It can only change form.

Why It's Important

Understanding that energy changes form but does not disappear has helped scientists to

- predict how energy will change form
- manage energy conversions in useful ways
- build and improve machines

Physical forces affect the movement of all matter on Earth and throughout the universe.

What makes the world go around? The answer is simple: forces. Forces allow you to walk across the room, and forces keep the stars together in galaxies. Consider the forces acting on the rafts below. The rushing water is pushing the rafts forward. The force from the people paddling helps to steer the rafts.

What It Means

A **force** is a push or a pull. Every time you push or pull an object, you're applying a force to that object, whether or not the object moves. There are several forces—several pushes and pulls—acting on you right now. All these forces are necessary for you to do the things you do, even sitting and reading.

- You are already familiar with the force of gravity. **Gravity** is the force of attraction between two objects. Right now gravity is at work pulling you to Earth and Earth to you. The Moon stays in orbit around Earth because gravity holds it close.

- A contact force occurs when one object pushes or pulls another object by touching it. If you kick a soccer ball, for instance, you apply a contact force to the ball. You apply a contact force to a shopping cart that you push down a grocery aisle or a sled that you pull up a hill.

- **Friction** is the force that resists motion between two surfaces pressed together. If you've ever tried to walk on an icy sidewalk, you know how important friction can be. If you lightly rub your finger across a smooth page in a book and then across a piece of sandpaper, you can feel how the different surfaces produce different frictional forces. Which is easier to do?

- There are other forces at work in the world too. For example, a compass needle responds to the magnetic force exerted by Earth's magnetic field, and objects made of certain metals are attracted by magnets. In addition to magnetic forces, there are electrical forces operating between particles and between objects. For example, you can demonstrate electrical forces by rubbing an inflated balloon on your hair. The balloon will then stick to your head or to a wall without additional means of support.

Why It's Important

Although some of these forces are more obvious than others, physical forces at work in the world are necessary for you to do the things you do. Understanding forces allows scientists to

- predict how objects will move
- design machines that perform complex tasks
- predict where planets and stars will be in the sky from one night to the next

The Nature of Science

You may think of science as a body of knowledge or a collection of facts. More important, however, science is an active process that involves certain ways of looking at the world.

Scientific Habits of Mind

Scientists are curious. They are always asking questions. Scientists have asked questions such as, "What is the smallest form of matter?" and "How do the smallest particles behave?" These and other important questions are being investigated by scientists around the world.

Scientists are observant. They are always looking closely at the world around them. Scientists once thought the smallest parts of atoms were protons, neutrons, and electrons. Later, protons and neutrons were found to be made of even smaller particles called quarks.

Scientists are creative. They draw on what they know to form possible explanations for a pattern, an event, or an interesting phenomenon that they have observed. Then scientists create a plan for testing their ideas.

Scientists are skeptical. Scientists don't accept an explanation or answer unless it is based on evidence and logical reasoning. They continually question their own conclusions and the conclusions suggested by other scientists. Scientists trust only evidence that is confirmed by other people or methods.

Scientists cannot always make observations with their own eyes. They have developed technology, such as this particle detector, to help them gather information about the smallest particles of matter.

Scientists ask questions about the physical world and seek answers through carefully controlled procedures. Here a researcher works with supercooled magnets.

Science Processes at Work

You can think of science as a continuous cycle of asking and seeking answers to questions about the world. Although there are many processes that scientists use, scientists typically do each of the following:

- Observe and ask a question
- Determine what is known
- Investigate
- Interpret results
- Share results

Observe and Ask a Question

It may surprise you that asking questions is an important skill. A scientific process may start when a scientist asks a question. Perhaps scientists observe an event or a process that they don't understand, or perhaps answering one question leads to another.

Determine What Is Known

When beginning an inquiry, scientists find out what is already known about a question. They study results from other scientific investigations, read journals, and talk with other scientists. A scientist working on subatomic particles is most likely a member of a large team using sophisticated equipment. Before beginning original research, the team analyzes results from previous studies.

Investigate

Investigating is the process of collecting evidence. Two important ways of investigating are observing and experimenting.

Observing is the act of noting and recording an event, a characteristic, or anything else detected with an instrument or with the senses. A researcher may study the properties of a substance by handling it, finding its mass, warming or cooling it, stretching it, and so on. For information about the behavior of subatomic particles, however, a researcher may rely on technology such as scanning tunneling microscopes, which produce images of structures that cannot be seen with the eye.

An **experiment** is an organized procedure to study something under controlled conditions. In order to study the effect of wing shape on the motion of a glider, for instance, a researcher would need to conduct controlled studies in which gliders made of the same materials and with the same masses differed only in the shape of their wings.

Scanning tunneling microscopes create images that allow scientists to observe molecular structure.

Physical chemists have found a way to observe chemical reactions at the atomic level. Using lasers, they can watch bonds breaking and new bonds forming.

Forming hypotheses and making predictions are two of the skills involved in scientific investigations. A **hypothesis** is a tentative explanation for an observation, a phenomenon, or a scientific problem that can be tested by further investigation. For example, in the mid-1800s astronomers noticed that the planet Uranus departed slightly from its expected orbit. One astronomer hypothesized that the irregularities in the planet's orbit were due to the gravitational effect of another planet—one that had not yet been detected. A **prediction** is an expectation of what will be observed or what will happen. A prediction can be used to test a hypothesis. The astronomers predicted that they would discover a new planet in the position calculated, and their prediction was confirmed with the discovery of the planet Neptune.

Interpret Results

As scientists investigate, they analyze their evidence, or data, and begin to draw conclusions. **Analyzing data** involves looking at the evidence gathered through observations or experiments and trying to identify any patterns that might exist in the data. Scientists often need to make additional observations or perform more experiments before they are sure of their conclusions. Many times scientists make new predictions or revise their hypotheses.

Often scientists use computers to help them analyze data. Computers reveal patterns that might otherwise be missed.

Scientists use computers to create models of objects or processes they are studying. This model shows carbon atoms forming a sphere.

Share Results

An important part of scientific investigation is sharing results of experiments. Scientists read and publish in journals and attend conferences to communicate with other scientists around the world. Sharing data and procedures gives them a way to test one another's results. They also share results with the public through newspapers, television, and other media.

The Nature of Technology

When you think of technology, you may think of cars, computers, and cell phones, as well as refrigerators, radios, and bicycles. Technology is not only the machines and devices that make modern lives easier, however. It is also a process in which new methods and devices are created. Technology makes use of scientific knowledge to design solutions to real-world problems.

Science and Technology

Science and technology go hand in hand. Each depends upon the other. Even designing a device as simple as a toaster requires knowledge of how heat flows and which materials are the best conductors of heat. Just as technology based on scientific knowledge makes our lives easier, some technology is used to advance scientific inquiry itself. For example, researchers use a number of specialized instruments to help them collect data. Microscopes, telescopes, spectrographs, and computers are just a few of the tools that help scientists learn more about the world. The more information these tools provide, the more devices can be developed to aid scientific research and to improve modern lives.

The Process of Technological Design

The process of technology involves many choices. For example, how does an automobile engineer design a better car? Is a better car faster? safer? cheaper? Before designing any new machine, the engineer must decide exactly what he or she wants the machine to do as well as what may be given up for the machine to do it. A faster car may get people to their destinations more quickly, but it may cost more and be less safe. As you study the technological process, think about all the choices that were made to build the technologies you use.

Identify a Need

Successful technology fills a need; it helps us perform a task we need or want to do. For example, as more cars appear on the road, noise and air pollution become serious threats to the environment and to people's health. Gas consumption also depletes precious petroleum resources. There is a need to find a fuel source for a car that will not pollute the air and that will never run out.

Design and Develop

Hydrogen fuel cells are a potential solution to this need. These cells combine hydrogen and oxygen into water, producing electricity in the process. Engineers have found a way to make fuel cells small enough to fit into a car, yet able to produce enough electricity to power an electric motor. Before arriving at this final design, engineers tried many others.

Test and Improve

Just because a technology works doesn't mean it cannot be improved. A fuel-cell-powered car has been driven from San Francisco to Washington, D.C., but it probably will be a while before it's in dealer showrooms. Engineers won't know how these cars will perform until they're driven in real-world conditions. Engineers also won't know if the average driver will be able to handle the necessary maintenance on the car until the car is made available to ordinary drivers. Improvements in the future may well bring cars powered by fuel cells into garages everywhere.

Using McDougal Littell Science

Reading Text and Visuals

This book is organized to help you learn. Use these boxed pointers as a path to help you learn and remember the **Big Ideas** and **Key Concepts**.

Take notes.

Use the strategies on the **Getting Ready to Learn** page.

Read the Big Idea.

As you read **Key Concepts** for the chapter, relate them to **the Big Idea**.

CHAPTER 2

Getting Ready to Learn

CHAPTER

2 Circui Electr

the **BIG** idea

Circuits control the flow of electric charge.

Key Concepts

SECTION 2.1 Charge needs a continuous path to flow.
Learn how circuits are used to control the flow of charge.

SECTION 2.2 Circuits make electric current useful.
Learn about series circuits and parallel circuits.

SECTION 2.3 Electronic technology is based on circuits.
Learn about computers and other electronic devices.

Internet Preview

CLASSZONE.COM
Chapter 2 online resources: Content Review, Simulation, Visualization, two Resource Centers, Math Tutorial, Test Practice

◄ **CONCEPT REVIEW**

• Energy can change from one form to another.
• Energy can move from one place to another.
• Current is the flow of charge through a conductor.

◄ **VOCABULARY REVIEW**

electric current p. 28
electric potential p. 18
conductor p. 22
resistance p. 23
ampere p. 29

CONTENT REVIEW
CLASSZONE.COM
Review concepts and vocabulary.

▶ **TAKING NOTES**

OUTLINE

As you read, copy the headings on your paper in the form of an outline. Then add notes in your own words that summarize what you read.

VOCABULARY STRATEGY

Write each new vocabulary term in the center of a **frame game diagram**. Decide what information to frame it with. Use examples, descriptions, parts, sentences that use the term in context, or pictures. You can change the frame to fit each term.

See the Note-Taking Handbook on pages R45–R51.

SCIENCE NOTEBOOK

I. ELECTRIC CHARGE FLOWS IN A LOOP.
  A. THE PARTS OF A CIRCUIT
    1. voltage source
    2. connection
    3. electrical device
    4. switch

Electrical device		
Part of a circuit	RESISTOR	Light bulb is an example
	Slows the flow of charge	

Read each heading.

See how it fits in the outline of the chapter.

2.1

KEY CONCEPT

Charge needs a continuous path to flow.

◀ **BEFORE,** you learned

- Current is the flow of charge
- Voltage is a measure of electric potential
- Materials affect the movement of charge

▶ **NOW,** you will learn

- About the parts of a circuit
- How a circuit functions
- How safety devices stop current

Remember what you know.

Think about concepts you learned earlier and preview what you'll learn now.

VOCABULARY

circuit p. 43
resistor p. 44
short circuit p. 46

EXPLORE Circuits

How can you light the bulb?

PROCEDURE

1. Tape one end of a strip of foil to the negative terminal, or the flat end, of the battery. Tape the other end of the foil to the tip at the base of the light bulb, as shown.

2. Tape the second strip of foil to the positive terminal, or the raised end, of the battery.

3. Find a way to make the bulb light.

WHAT DO YOU THINK?
- How did you make the bulb light?
- Can you find other arrangements that make the bulb light?

MATERIALS
- 2 strips of aluminum foil
- electrical tape
- D cell (battery)
- light bulb

Try the activities.

They will introduce you to science concepts.

VOCABULARY
Use a frame game diagram to record the term *circuit* in your notebook.

Electric charge flows in a loop.

In the last chapter, you read that current is electric charge that flows from one place to another. Charge does not flow continuously through a material unless the material forms a closed path, or loop. A **circuit** is a closed path through which a continuous charge can flow. The path is provided by a low-resistance material, or conductor, usually wire. Circuits are designed to do specific jobs, such as light a bulb.

Circuits can be found all around you and serve many different purposes. In this chapter, you will read about simple circuits, such as the ones in flashlights, and more complex circuits, such as the ones that run toys, cameras, computers, and more.

CHECK YOUR READING How are circuits related to current?

Learn the vocabulary.

Take notes on each term.

Answer the questions.

Check Your Reading questions will help you remember what you read.

Reading Text and Visuals

Open and Closed Circuits

Current in a circuit is similar to water running through a hose. The flow of charge differs from the flow of water in an important way, however. The water does not require a closed path to flow. If you cut the hose, the water continues to flow. If you cut a wire, the charge stops flowing.

Batteries have connections at both ends so that charge can follow a closed path to and from the battery. The cords that you see on appliances might look like single cords but actually contain at least two wires. The wires connect the device to a power plant and back to make a closed path.

Switches work by opening and closing the circuit. A switch that is on closes the circuit and allows charge to flow through the electrical devices. A switch that is off opens the circuit and stops the current.

 REMINDER
Current requires a closed loop.

CHECK YOUR READING How are switches used to control the flow of charge through a circuit?

Standard symbols are used to represent the parts of a circuit. Some common symbols are shown in the circuit diagrams below. The diagrams represent the circuit shown on page 44 with the switch in both open and closed positions. Electricians and architects use diagrams such as these to plan the wiring of a building.

Read one paragraph at a time.

Look for a topic sentence that explains the main idea of the paragraph. Figure out how the details relate to that idea. One paragraph might have several important ideas; you may have to reread to understand.

Answer the questions.

Check Your Reading questions will help you remember what you read.

Study the visuals.

- Read the title.
- Read all labels and captions.
- Figure out what the picture is showing. Notice colors, arrows, and lines.

Circuit Diagrams

Symbols are used to represent the parts of a circuit. The circuit diagrams below show the circuit from page 44 in both an open and closed position.

Key	
$+\|-$	cell
$+\|\cdot\|-$	2-cell battery
$+\|\cdot\|\cdot\|-$	4-cell battery
$\multimap\ \circ-$	open switch
light bulb	light bulb

open switch = off   closed switch = on

READING VISUALS Would charge flow through the circuit diagrammed on the left? Why or why not?

Doing Labs

To understand science, you have to see it in action. Doing labs helps you understand how things really work.

① Read the entire lab first.

② Form a hypothesis.

③ Follow the procedure.

④ Record the data.

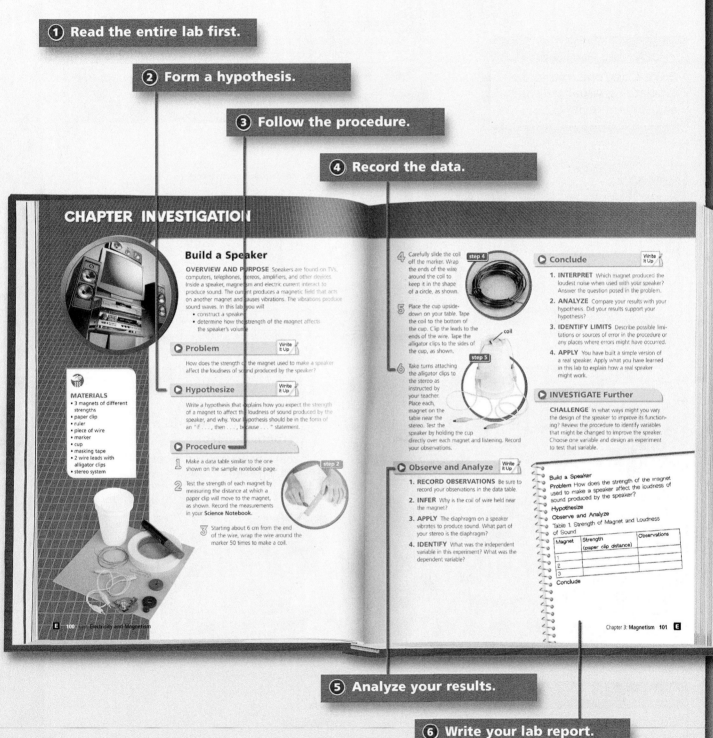

CHAPTER INVESTIGATION

Build a Speaker

OVERVIEW AND PURPOSE Speakers are found on TVs, computers, telephones, stereos, amplifiers, and other devices. Inside a speaker, magnetism and electric current interact to produce sound. The current produces a magnetic field that acts on another magnet and causes vibrations. The vibrations produce sound waves. In this lab you will
- construct a speaker
- determine how the strength of the magnet affects the speaker's volume

○ **Problem** [Write It Up]

How does the strength of the magnet used to make a speaker affect the loudness of sound produced by the speaker?

○ **Hypothesize** [Write It Up]

Write a hypothesis that explains how you expect the strength of a magnet to affect the loudness of sound produced by the speaker, and why. Your hypothesis should be in the form of an "if . . . , then . . . , because . . . " statement.

○ **Procedure**

1. Make a data table similar to the one shown on the sample notebook page.

2. Test the strength of each magnet by measuring the distance at which a paper clip will move to the magnet, as shown. Record the measurements in your **Science Notebook**.

3. Starting about 6 cm from the end of the wire, wrap the wire around the marker 50 times to make a coil.

MATERIALS
- 3 magnets of different strengths
- paper clip
- ruler
- piece of wire
- marker
- cup
- masking tape
- 2 wire leads with alligator clips
- stereo system

4. Carefully slide the coil off the marker. Wrap the ends of the wire around the coil to keep it in the shape of a circle, as shown.

5. Place the cup upside-down on your table. Tape the coil to the bottom of the cup. Clip the leads to the ends of the wire. Tape the alligator clips to the sides of the cup, as shown.

6. Take turns attaching the alligator clips to the stereo as instructed by your teacher. Place each magnet on the table near the stereo. Test the speaker by holding the cup directly over each magnet and listening. Record your observations.

○ **Observe and Analyze** [Write It Up]

1. **RECORD OBSERVATIONS** Be sure to record your observations in the data table.

2. **INFER** Why is the coil of wire held near the magnet?

3. **APPLY** The diaphragm on a speaker vibrates to produce sound. What part of your stereo is the diaphragm?

4. **IDENTIFY** What was the independent variable in this experiment? What was the dependent variable?

○ **Conclude** [Write It Up]

1. **INTERPRET** Which magnet produced the loudest noise when used with your speaker? Answer the question posed in the problem.

2. **ANALYZE** Compare your results with your hypothesis. Did your results support your hypothesis?

3. **IDENTIFY LIMITS** Describe possible limitations or sources of error in the procedure or any places where errors might have occurred.

4. **APPLY** You have built a simple version of a real speaker. Apply what you have learned in this lab to explain how a real speaker might work.

○ **INVESTIGATE Further**

CHALLENGE In what ways might you vary the design of the speaker to improve its functioning? Review the procedure to identify variables that might be changed to improve the speaker. Choose one variable and design an experiment to test that variable.

Build a Speaker
Problem How does the strength of the magnet used to make a speaker affect the loudness of sound produced by the speaker?
Hypothesize
Observe and Analyze
Table 1. Strength of Magnet and Loudness of Sound

Magnet	Strength (paper clip distance)	Observations
1		
2		
3		

Conclude

⑤ Analyze your results.

⑥ Write your lab report.

Using Technology

The Internet is a great source of up-to-date science. The ClassZone Website and SciLinks have exciting sites for you to explore. Video clips and simulations can make science come alive.

Look for red banners.

Go to **ClassZone.com** to see simulations, visualizations, and content review.

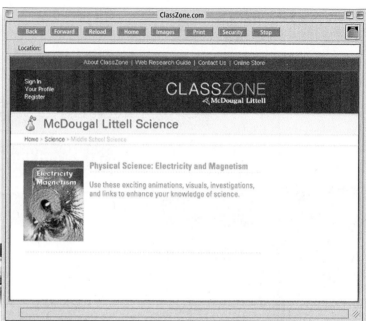

Physical Science: Electricity and Magnetism

Use these exciting animations, visuals, investigations, and links to enhance your knowledge of science.

Watch the video.

See science at work in the **Scientific American Frontiers video.**

Look up SciLinks.

Go to **scilinks.org** to explore the topic.

Electronic Circuits **CODE: MDL066**

Electricity and Magnetism
Contents Overview

Unit Features

1 Electricity   6

the **BIG** idea

Moving electric charges
transfer energy.

2 Circuits and Electronics   40

the **BIG** idea

Circuits control the flow of
electric charge.

3 Magnetism   76

the **BIG** idea

Current can produce magnetism,
and magnetism can produce current.

Electronics in
Music

How are
electronics changing
the way we make
and listen to music?

SCIENTIFIC AMERICAN FRONTIERS

View the video segment "Toy Symphony" to learn about some creative new ways in which music and electronics can be combined.

The quality of amplified sound waves can be controlled using electronics. Controls on this soundboard are adjusted in preparation for an outdoor concert.

Catching a Sound Wave

Everyone knows that music and electronics go together. If you want to hear music, you turn on a radio or TV, choose a CD or DVD to play, or listen to a computer file downloaded in MP3. All of these formats use electronics to record, play, and amplify music. Some of the most recent developments in music also use electronics to produce the music in the first place. For example, the orchestral music playing in the background of the last blockbuster movie you saw may not have been played by an orchestra at all. It may have been produced electronically on a computer.

Music consists of sound, and sound is a wave. Inside your TV or stereo equipment, electronic circuits represent sound waves as analog signals or digital signals. In analog recordings a peak in the original sound wave corresponds to a peak in the current. Radio and TV broadcasts are usually analog signals. The sound wave is converted to electromagnetic waves sent out through the air. Your radio or TV set receives these waves and converts them back to a sound wave.

In digital sound recordings the system samples the incoming sound wave at frequent intervals of time, such as 44,100 times per second. The system measures the height of each wave and assigns it a number. The numbers form a digital signal. This information can then be stored and transmitted. The playback electronics, such as CD players and DVD players, convert the signal back to a sound wave for you to hear.

Digital Devices

In a compact disc (CD), the numbers representing the sound wave are coded into a series of microscopic pits in a long spiral track burned into the plastic of the CD. A laser beam scans the track and reads the pits, converting the data back into numbers. This information is then converted into sound waves by an electronic circuit in the CD player. CDs can store up to 74 minutes of music because the pits are only a few millionths of a meter in size. Digital videodiscs (DVDs) often have several layers, each with a separate data

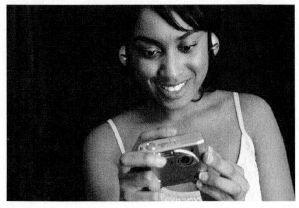

MP3 players store digital files that are compressed in size.

track, and use even smaller tracks and pits than CDs use. As a result, a DVD can store seven times as much information as a CD.

The amount of computer space needed to represent a song in normal digital format is too large to store very many songs on a single device. However, the development of a compression program called MP3 decreases the size of a typical song to one-tenth its original size. This enables you to buy and download a song from the Internet in minutes instead of hours and store files on your computer or MP3 player without taking up too much space.

Making Music

These advances in recording and playing music enables you to listen to music, whatever your taste in music happens to be. Electronic technology also allows you to change the music or even generate your own music, as shown in the video. Recording engineers used to work with large electronic consoles with hundreds of switches in order to blend different singers and background

SCIENTIFIC AMERICAN FRONTIERS

View the "Toy Symphony" segment of your *Scientific American Frontiers* video to learn how electronic devices allow people to interact with music in new ways.

IN THIS SCENE FROM THE VIDEO ◉
Kids play with Beatbugs at MIT's Media Lab.

PLAYING WITH SOUNDS At the Massachusetts Institute of Technology (MIT) Media Lab, Tod Machover and his colleagues have invented several new musical instruments that are based on electronics. One such invention is the hyperviolin,

demonstrated by concert violinist Joshua Bell. As Joshua plays the violin, a computer registers the movements of the bow and produces new and different sounds from the movements. Other musical electronic devices in the lab are designed to allow someone with little or no experience with an instrument to play and compose music.

With Beatbugs—small interactive devices—kids can play music and collaborate with others. They can also compose and edit their own music. Using new computer software, a ten-year-old boy was able to compose an entire symphony played by the German Symphony Orchestra.

Home recording studios are possible because of new electronic technology.

instruments or to add special effects such as echoes or distortion. Now this can all be done on a laptop computer, using the Musical Instrument Digital Interface (MIDI).

MIDI technology is an advancement in digital technology. Whereas CD, DVD, and MP3 files represent the sound waves themselves, MIDI files represent the instructions for another device—such as an electronic instrument—to play the music. With MIDI, you can connect an electronic keyboard directly to a computer and compose and edit your own music, layer in the sounds of different instruments, and dub in special effects. Once you understand how to use electronics to produce the sound waves you want, you can become your own favorite band.

?UNANSWERED Questions

Every year, scientists develop new technologies affecting the way we produce and listen to music. As advances in music technology are made, new question arise.

- Are there electronic sounds that no one has heard before?
- How will the development of music technology affect who is producing music?
- What type of devices will people be using to listen to music in 50 years?

UNIT PROJECTS

As you study this unit, work alone or with a group on one of these projects.

Multimedia Presentation

Put together an informative presentation that explains how electric guitars work.

- Gather information about electric guitars. Learn how they use both electricity and magnetism.
- Give a presentation that uses mixed media, such as a computer slide show, model, poster, or tape recording.

Build a Radio

Build a working radio from simple materials.

- Using books or the Internet, find instructions for building a simple crystal radio.
- Collect the materials and assemble the radio. Modify the design of the radio to improve it.
- Demonstrate the radio to the class and explain how it works.

Design an Invention

Design an electronic invention.

- Select a purpose for your invention, such as a toy, a fan, or a burglar alarm. Write a paragraph that explains the purpose of your invention.
- Draw a sketch of your design and modify it if necessary.
- Make a pamphlet to advertise your invention. If possible, build the invention and include photographs of it in the pamphlet.

 CAREER CENTER
CLASSZONE.COM

Learn more about careers in music and computer science.

CHAPTER

Electricity

the **BIG** idea

Moving electric charges transfer energy.

> **What keeps this dragon glowing brightly?**

Key Concepts

SECTION
1.1 Materials can become electrically charged.
Learn how the movement of electrons builds static charges and how static charges are used in technology.

SECTION
1.2 Charges can move from one place to another.
Learn what factors control the movement of charges.

SECTION
1.3 Electric current is a flow of charge.
Learn how electric current is measured and how it can be produced.

Internet Preview

CLASSZONE.COM

Chapter 1 online resources: Content Review, two Simulations, two Resource Centers, Math Tutorial, Test Practice.

E 6 Unit: Electricity and Magnetism

How Do the Pieces of Tape Interact?

Cut three strips of tape. Press two onto your shirt. Peel them off and hold them close to each other, without touching. Observe. Hold one of them close to the third strip. Observe.

Observe and Think
How did the strips of tape behave in each case? Can you think of an explanation?

Why Does the Water React Differently?

Open a faucet just enough to let flow a thin stream of water. Run a comb through your hair a few times, and then hold it near the stream of water. Observe the behavior of the water. Touch the comb to the stream of water briefly and then hold it near the stream again.

Observe and Think How did the interaction of the comb and the stream change after you touched the comb to the water?

Internet Activity: Static Electricity

Go to **ClassZone.com** to learn more about materials and static electricity.

Observe and Think What role does the type of material play in static electricity?

Electricity Code: MDL065

Getting Ready to Learn

◀ CONCEPT REVIEW

- Matter is made of particles too small to see.
- Energy and matter can move from one place to another.
- Electromagnetic energy is one form of energy.

◀ VOCABULARY REVIEW

See Glossary for definitions.

atom

electron

joule

proton

ⓘ CONTENT REVIEW
CLASSZONE.COM
Review concepts and vocabulary.

▶ TAKING NOTES

COMBINATION NOTES

To take notes about a new concept, first make an informal outline of the information. Then make a sketch of the concept and label it so you can study it later.

VOCABULARY STRATEGY

Write each new vocabulary term in the center of a **four square** diagram. Write notes in the squares around each term. Include a definition, some characteristics, and some examples of the term. If possible, write some things that are not examples of the term.

See the Note-Taking Handbook on pages R45–R51.

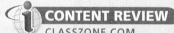

SCIENCE NOTEBOOK

<u>NOTES</u>
How static charges are built
- Contact
- Induction
- Charge polarization

charging by contact

Definition	Characteristics
imbalance of charge in material	results from movement of electrons; affected by type of material
STATIC CHARGE	
Examples	Nonexample
clinging laundry, doorknob shock, lightning	electricity from an electrical outlet

Materials can become electrically charged.

 BEFORE, you learned

- Atoms are made up of particles called protons, neutrons, and electrons
- Protons and electrons are electrically charged

 NOW, you will learn

- How charged particles behave
- How electric charges build up in materials
- How static electricity is used in technology

VOCABULARY

electric charge p. 10
electric field p. 10
static charge p. 11
induction p. 13

EXPLORE Static Electricity

How can materials interact electrically?

PROCEDURE

1. Hold the newspaper strips firmly together at one end and let the free ends hang down. Observe the strips.

2. Put the plastic bag over your other hand, like a mitten. Slide the plastic down the entire length of the strips and then let go. Repeat several times.

3. Notice how the strips of paper are hanging. Describe what you observe.

WHAT DO YOU THINK?

- How did the strips behave before step 2? How did they behave after step 2?
- How might you explain your observations?

MATERIALS
- 2 strips of newspaper
- plastic bag

Electric charge is a property of matter.

You are already familiar with electricity, static electricity, and magnetism. You know electricity as the source of power for many appliances, including lights, tools, and computers. Static electricity is what makes clothes stick together when they come out of a dryer and gives you a shock when you touch a metal doorknob on a dry, winter day. Magnetism can hold an invitation or report card on the door of your refrigerator.

You may not know, however, that electricity, static electricity, and magnetism are all related. All three are the result of a single property of matter—electric charge.

COMBINATION NOTES
As you read this section, write down important ideas about electric charge and static charges. Make sketches to help you remember these concepts.

The smallest unit of a material that still has the characteristics of that material is an atom or a molecule. A molecule is two or more atoms bonded together. Most of an atom's mass is concentrated in the nucleus at the center of the atom. The nucleus contains particles called protons and neutrons. Much smaller particles called electrons move at high speeds outside the nucleus.

Protons and electrons have electric charges. **Electric charge** is a property that allows an object to exert an electric force on another object without touching it. Recall that a force is a push or a pull. The space around a particle through which an electric charge can exert this force is called an **electric field.** The strength of the field is greater near the particle and weaker farther away.

All protons have a positive charge (+), and all electrons have a negative charge (–). Normally, an atom has an equal number of protons and electrons, so their charges balance each other, and the overall charge on the atom is neutral.

Particles with the same type of charge—positive or negative—are said to have like charges, and particles with different charges have unlike charges. Particles with like charges repel each other, that is, they push each other away. Particles with unlike charges attract each other, or pull on each other.

VOCABULARY
Make a four square diagram for the term *electric charge* and the other vocabulary terms in this section.

Electric Charge

Charged particles exert forces on each other through their electric fields.

Charged Particles
Electric charge can be either negative or positive.

The balloon and the cat's fur have unlike charges, so they attract each other.

① **Attraction**

Particles with unlike charges attract—pull on each other.

② **Repulsion**

Particles with like charges repel—push each other away.

 ⊖ = electron

 ⊕ = proton

 — = lines of force

READING VISUALS How do the force lines change when particles attract?

Static charges are caused by the movement of electrons.

You have read that protons and electrons have electric charges. Objects and materials can also have charges. A **static charge** is a buildup of electric charge in an object caused by the presence of many particles with the same charge. Ordinarily, the atoms that make up a material have a balance of protons and electrons. A material develops a static charge—or becomes charged—when it contains more of one type of charged particle than another.

If there are more protons than electrons in a material, the material has a positive charge. If there are more electrons than protons in a material, it has a negative charge. The amount of the charge depends on how many more electrons or protons there are. The total number of unbalanced positive or negative charges in an object is the net charge of the object. Net charge is measured in coulombs (KOO-LAHMZ). One coulomb is equivalent to more than 10^{19} electrons or protons.

Electrons can move easily from one atom to another. Protons cannot. For this reason, charges in materials usually result from the movement of electrons. The movement of electrons through a material is called conduction. If electrons move from one atom to another, the atom they move to develops a negative charge. The atom they move away from develops a positive charge. Atoms with either a positive or a negative charge are called ions.

A static charge can build up in an uncharged material when it touches or comes near a charged material. Static charges also build up when some types of uncharged materials come into contact with each other.

READING TIP

The word *static* comes from the Greek word *statos,* which means "standing."

REMINDER

10^{19} is the same as 1 followed by 19 zeros.

Charging by Contact

When two uncharged objects made of certain materials—such as rubber and glass—touch each other, electrons move from one material to the other. This process is called charging by contact. It can be demonstrated by a balloon and a glass rod, as shown below.

① At first, a balloon and a glass rod each have balanced, neutral charges.

② When they touch, electrons move from the rod to the balloon.

③ Afterwards, the balloon has a negative charge, and the rod has a positive charge.

metal globe

As the sphere takes on a negative charge, electrons spread out over this student's skin and hair. Because her hairs all have the same charge, they repel one another.

connection to globe

conveyor belt

source of electrons

A Van de Graaff generator is a device that builds up a strong static charge through contact. This device is shown at left. At the bottom of the device, a rubber conveyer belt rubs against a metal brush and picks up electrons. At the top, the belt rubs against metal connected to the sphere, transferring electrons to the sphere. As more and more electrons accumulate on the sphere, the sphere takes on a strong negative charge. In the photograph, the student touches the sphere as it is being charged. Some of the electrons spread across her arm to her head. The strands of her hair, which then all have a negative charge, repel one another.

CHECK YOUR READING How can a Van de Graaff generator make a person's hair stand on end?

How Materials Affect Static Charging

Charging by contact occurs when one material's electrons are attracted to another material more than they are attracted to their own. Scientists have determined from experience which materials are likely to give up or to accept electrons. For example, glass gives up electrons to wool. Wool accepts electrons from glass, but gives up electrons to rubber. The list at left indicates how some materials interact. Each material tends to give up electrons to anything below it on the list and to accept electrons from anything above it. The farther away two materials are from each other on the list, the stronger the interaction.

When you walk across a carpet, your body can become either positively or negatively charged. The type of charge depends on what materials the carpet and your shoes are made of. If you walk in shoes with rubber soles across a wool carpet, you will probably become negatively charged, because wool gives up electrons to rubber. But if you walk in wool slippers across a rubber mat, you will probably become positively charged.

Charging by Contact
skin
glass
hair
nylon
wool
fur
silk
paper
rubber
polyester

Materials higher on the list tend to give up electrons to materials lower on the list.

rubber

wool

Rubber soles on a wool carpet give a person a negative charge.

wool

rubber

Wool slippers on a rubber mat give a person a positive charge.

Charging by Induction

Charging can occur even when materials are not touching if one of the materials already has a charge. Remember that charged particles push and pull each other through their electric fields without touching. The pushing and pulling can cause a charge to build in another material. The first charge is said to induce the second charge. The buildup of a charge without direct contact is called **induction.**

READING **TiP**

Induce and *induction* both contain the Latin root *ducere,* which means "to lead."

Induction can produce a temporary static charge. Consider what happens when a glass rod with a negative charge is brought near a balloon, as shown below. The unbalanced electrons in the rod repel the electrons in the material of the balloon. Many electrons move to the side of the balloon that is farthest away from the rod. The side of the balloon that has more electrons becomes negatively charged. The side of the balloon with fewer electrons becomes positively charged. When the rod moves away, the electrons spread out evenly once again.

1 At first, the rod has a negative charge and the balloon has a balanced charge.

2 When the rod comes close to the balloon, electrons in the balloon move away from the rod.

3 When the rod moves away, electrons in the balloon spread out evenly as before.

If the electrons cannot return to their original distribution, however, induction can leave an object with a stable static charge. For example, if a negatively charged rod approaches two balloons that are touching each other, electrons will move to the balloon farther from the rod. If the balloons are then separated, preventing the electrons from moving again, the balloon with more electrons will have a negative charge and the one with fewer electrons will have a positive charge. When the rod is taken away, the balloons keep their new charges.

1 At first, the rod has a negative charge and the balloons have balanced charges.

2 As the rod approaches, electrons move to the balloon farther away.

3 If the balloons are then separated, the balloons retain their charges.

Charge Polarization

Induction can build a charge by changing the position of electrons, even when electrons do not move between atoms. Have you ever charged a balloon by rubbing it on your head, and then stuck the balloon to a wall? When you bring the balloon close to the wall, the balloon's negative charge pushes against the electrons in the wall. If the electrons cannot easily move away from their atoms, the negative charges within the atoms may shift to the side away from the balloon. When this happens, the atoms are said to be polarized. The surface of the wall becomes positively charged, and the negatively charged balloon sticks to it.

surface of wall

surface of wall

① Before the charged balloon comes near the wall, the atoms in the surface of the wall are not polarized.

② As the balloon nears the wall, atoms in the surface of the wall become polarized and attract the balloon.

INVESTIGATE Making a Static Detector

How can you detect a static electric charge?

PROCEDURE

① Straighten one end of the paper clip and insert it through the hole in the cup. Use clay to hold the paper clip in place. Stick the ball of foil onto the straight end. Hang both foil strips from the hook end.

② Give the balloon a static charge by rubbing it over your hair. Slowly bring the balloon near the ball of foil without letting them touch. Observe what happens to the foil strips inside the cup.

WHAT DO YOU THINK?

• What happened to the strips hanging inside the cup when the charged balloon came near the ball of foil?

• How can you explain what you observed?

CHALLENGE Suppose the balloon had the opposite charge of the one you gave it. What would happen to the strips if you brought the balloon near the ball of foil? Explain your answer.

SKILL FOCUS
Inferring

MATERIALS
• metal paper clip
• clear plastic cup with hole
• modeling clay
• ball of foil
• 2 strips of foil
• inflated balloon

TIME
20 minutes

Technology uses static electricity.

Static charges can be useful in technology. An example is the photocopy machine. Photocopiers run on electricity that comes to them through wires from the power plant. But static charges play an important role in how they work.

How a Photocopier Works

A photocopier uses static charges to make copies.

Input An original document goes into the copier. A bright light shines on the page.

mirror

toner cartridge

original

Inside the Copier The letters or images are transferred from the original to the copy, as shown in the box at right.

lamp

drum 1

drum 2

heating element

Output Heat fixes the toner to the paper, creating a permanent copy of the original.

paper

Inside the Copier

light —

1 A mirror reflects light from white areas of the original onto drum 1, which is positively charged. These lighted areas of the drum become negatively charged.

toner

2 Negatively charged toner (powdered ink) is attracted to the positive areas of drum 1 in the pattern of the original.

positively charged paper

3 Drum 1 rolls against a fresh, positively charged piece of paper on drum 2. The toner on drum 1 sticks to the paper.

READING VISUALS Why does the copy have the same pattern of light and dark areas as the original?

Static electricity is also used in making cars. When new cars are painted, the paint is given an electric charge and then sprayed onto the car in a fine mist. The tiny droplets of paint stick to the car more firmly than they would without the charge. This process results in a coat of paint that is very even and smooth.

Another example of the use of static electricity in technology is a device called an electrostatic air filter. This device cleans air inside buildings with the help of static charges. The filter gives a static charge to pollen, dust, germs, and other particles in the air. Then an oppositely charged plate inside the filter attracts these particles, pulling them out of the air. Larger versions of electrostatic filters are used to remove pollutants from industrial smokestacks.

 CHECK YOUR READING   How can static charges help clean air?

1.1 Review

KEY CONCEPTS

1. How do a positive and a negative particle interact?

2. Describe how the movement of electrons between two objects with balanced charges could cause the buildup of electric charge in both objects.

3. Describe one technological use of static electricity.

CRITICAL THINKING

4. **Infer** A sock and a shirt from the dryer stick together. What does this tell you about the charges on the sock and shirt?

5. **Analyze** You walk over a rug and get a shock from a door-knob. What do the materials of the rug and the shoes have to do with the type of charge your body had?

CHALLENGE

6. **Apply** Assume you start with a negatively charged rod and two balloons. Describe a series of steps you could take to create a positively charged balloon, pick up negatively charged powder with the balloon, and drop the powder from the balloon.

Electric Eels

An electric eel is a slow-moving fish with no teeth and poor eyesight. It lives in the murky waters of muddy rivers in South America. Instead of the senses that most animals use—vision, hearing, smell, and touch—an electric eel uses electricity to find its next meal. Since the fish that it eats often can swim much faster than the eel, it also uses electricity to catch its prey.

Electric Sense

An electric eel actually has three pairs of electric organs in its body. Two of them build electric charge for stunning prey and for self-defense. The third electric organ builds a smaller charge that helps in finding prey. The charge produces an electric field around the eel. Special sense organs on its body detect small changes in the electric field caused by nearby fish and other animals.

Shocking Organs

The electric eel builds an electric charge with a series of thousands of cells called electrocytes. Every cell in the series has a positive end and a negative end. Each electrocyte builds only a small charge. However, when all of the cells combine their charge, they can produce about five times as much electricity as a standard electrical outlet in a house. The charge is strong enough to paralyze or kill a human. Typically, though, the charge is used to stun or kill small fish, which the eel then swallows whole. Electric charge can also be used to scare away predators.

EXPLORE

1. **INFER** Electric eels live for 10 to 20 years, developing a stronger shock as they grow older. What could account for this increase in electric charge?

2. **CHALLENGE** Sharks and other animals use electricity also. Use the library or Internet to find out how.

An electric eel (Electrophorus electricus) can deliver a jolt five times as powerful as an electrical outlet.

Charges can move from one place to another.

◁ **BEFORE,** you learned

- Static charges are built up by the separation of electrons from protons
- Materials affect how static charges are built up
- Energy is the ability to cause change

▷ **NOW,** you will learn

- How charges move
- How charges store energy
- How differences in materials affect the movement of charges

VOCABULARY

electric potential p. 19
volt p. 19
conductor p. 22
insulator p. 22
resistance p. 23
ohm p. 23
grounding p. 25

EXPLORE Static Discharge

How can you observe electrical energy?

PROCEDURE

① Rub the balloon against the wool cloth several times to give the balloon a static charge.

② Slowly bring the balloon toward the middle part of the fluorescent bulb until a spark jumps between them.

WHAT DO YOU THINK?

- What happened in the fluorescent bulb when the spark jumped?
- How might you explain this observation?

MATERIALS

- inflated balloon
- wool cloth
- fluorescent light bulb

Static charges have potential energy.

You have read how a static charge is built up in an object such as a balloon. Once it is built up, the charge can stay where it is indefinitely. However, the charge can also move to a new location. The movement of a static charge out of an object is known as static discharge. When a charge moves, it transfers energy that can be used to do work.

What causes a charge to move is the same thing that builds up a charge in the first place—that is, the force of attraction or repulsion between charged particles. For example, suppose an object with a negative charge touches an object with a positive charge. The attraction of the unbalanced electrons in the first object to the unbalanced protons in the second object can cause the electrons to move to the second object.

○ **REMINDER**

Energy can be either kinetic (energy of motion) or potential (stored energy). Energy is measured in joules.

◎ **CHECK YOUR READING** What can cause a charge to move?

Electric Potential Energy

Potential energy is stored energy an object may have because of its position. Water in a tower has gravitational potential energy because it is high above the ground. The kinetic energy—energy of motion—used to lift the water to the top of the tower is stored as potential energy. If you open a pipe below the tower, the water moves downward and its potential energy is converted back into kinetic energy.

Similarly, electric potential energy is the energy a charged particle has due to its position in an electric field. Because like charges repel, for example, it takes energy to push a charged particle closer to another particle with a like charge. That energy is stored as the electric potential energy of the first particle. When the particle is free to move again, it quickly moves away, and its electric potential energy is converted back into kinetic energy.

When water moves downward out of a tower and some of its potential energy is converted into kinetic energy, its potential energy decreases. Similarly, when a charged particle moves away from a particle with a like charge, its electric potential energy decreases. The water and the particle both move from a state of higher potential energy to one of lower potential energy.

Like water in a tower, a static charge has potential energy. Just as gravity moves water down the supply pipe attached under the tank, the electric potential energy of a charge moves the charge along an electrical pathway.

Electric Potential

To push a charged particle closer to another particle with the same charge takes a certain amount of energy. To push two particles into the same position near that particle takes twice as much energy, and the two particles together have twice as much electric potential energy as the single particle. Although the amount of potential energy is higher, the amount of energy per unit charge at that position stays the same. **Electric potential** is the amount of electric potential energy per unit charge at a certain position in an electric field.

Electric potential is measured in units called volts, and voltage is another term for electric potential. A potential of one **volt** is equal to one joule of energy per coulomb of charge.

Just as water will not flow between two towers of the same height, a charge will not move between two positions with the same electric potential. For a charge to move, there must be a difference in potential between the two positions.

Charge Movement

When water moves from a higher to a lower position, some of its potential energy is used to move it. Along the way, some of its potential energy can be used to do other work, such as turning a water wheel. Similarly, when a charge moves, some of its electric potential energy is used in moving the charge and some of it can be used to do other work. For example, moving an electric charge through a material can cause the material to heat up, as in a burner on an electric stove.

You can see how a moving charge transfers energy when you get a shock from static electricity. As you walk across a rug, a charge builds up on your body. Once the charge is built up, it cannot move until you come in contact with something else. When you reach out to touch a doorknob, the charge has a path to follow. The electric potential energy of the charge moves the charge from you to the doorknob.

Why do you get a shock? Recall that the force of attraction or repulsion between charged particles is stronger when they are close together. As your hand gets closer to the doorknob, the electric potential of the static charge increases. At a certain point, the difference in electric potential between you and the doorknob is great enough to move the charge through the air to the doorknob. As the charge moves, some of its potential energy is changed into the heat, light, and sound of a spark.

 CHECK YOUR READING What two factors determine whether a static charge will move?

Lightning

RESOURCE CENTER
CLASSZONE.COM

Find out more about lightning and lightning safety.

The shock you get from a doorknob is a small-scale version of lightning. Lightning is a high-energy static discharge. This static electricity is caused by storm clouds. Lightning comes from the electric potential of millions of volts, which releases large amounts of energy in the form of light, heat, and sound. As you read about how lightning forms, follow the steps in the illustration on page 21.

➊ **Charge Separation** Particles of moisture inside a cloud collide with the air and with each other, causing the particles to become electrically charged. Wind and gravity separate charges, carrying the heavier, negatively charged particles to the bottom of the cloud and the lighter, positively charged particles to the top of the cloud.

➋ **Charge Buildup** Through induction, the negatively charged particles at the bottom of the cloud repel electrons in the ground, causing the surface of the ground to build up a positive charge.

➌ **Static Discharge** When the electric potential, or voltage, created by the difference in charges is large enough, the negative charge moves from the cloud to the ground. The energy released by the discharge produces the flash of lightning and the sound of thunder.

How Lightning Forms

Lightning is a type of static discharge. Storm clouds may develop very large charges, each with an electric potential of millions of volts.

① Charge Separation

Collisions between particles in storm clouds separate charges. Negatively charged particles collect at the bottom of the cloud.

② Charge Buildup

The negatively charged bottom part of the cloud induces a positive charge in the surface of the ground.

③ Static Discharge

The charge jumps through the air to the ground. Energy released by the discharge causes thunder and lightning.

READING VISUALS How is lightning like the shock you can get from a doorknob? How is it different?

Materials affect charge movement.

COMBINATION NOTES
Make notes on the different ways materials can affect charge movement. Use sketches to help explain the concepts.

After you walk across a carpet, a charge on your skin has no place to go until you touch or come very close to something. That is because an electric charge cannot move easily through air. However, a charge can move easily through the metal of a doorknob.

Conductors and Insulators

A material that allows an electric charge to pass through it easily is called a **conductor.** Metals such as iron, steel, copper, and aluminum are good conductors. Most wire used to carry a charge is made of copper, which conducts very well.

A material that does not easily allow a charge to pass through it is called an **insulator.** Plastic and rubber are good insulators. Many types of electric wire are covered with plastic, which insulates well. The plastic allows a charge to be conducted from one end of the wire to the other, but not through the sides of the wire. Insulators are also important in electrical safety, because they keep charges away from the body.

CHECK YOUR READING What is the difference between a conductor and an insulator?

INVESTIGATE Conductors and Insulators

What materials conduct electricity?

PROCEDURE

1. Use tape to connect the battery, wires, and bulb holder as shown in the photograph. Make sure that the wires connected to the battery stay in full contact with the metal parts on either end. Test the bulb and the battery by touching the free ends of wire together. The bulb should light up.

2. Test each object in turn by touching it simultaneously with both free ends of wire. Make sure the ends of wire do not touch each other.

WHAT DO YOU THINK?

- Which objects allowed the light bulb to light up when the wires touched them? Which did not?

- How can you explain the difference between the two groups of objects?

CHALLENGE Do any of the materials you tested seem to conduct a charge better than other conductors? How could you use the setup you have to compare the degree of conducting ability of materials?

SKILL FOCUS
Interpreting data

MATERIALS
- D cell (battery)
- 3 pieces of low-voltage wire
- duct tape
- flashlight bulb
- bulb holder
- objects of different materials

TIME
20 minutes

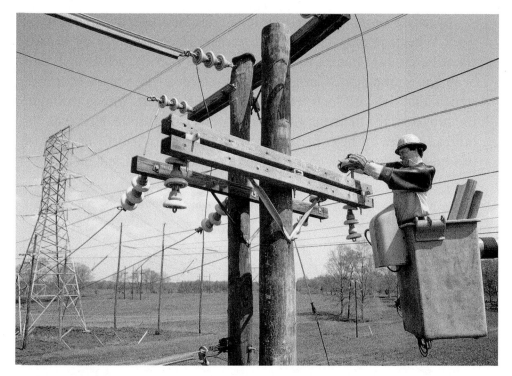

Electrons can move freely in a material with low resistance, such as the copper wire in these power lines. Electrons cannot move freely in a material with high resistance, such as the ceramic insulator this worker is putting in place or his safety gloves.

Resistance

Think about the difference between walking through air and walking through waist-deep water. The water resists your movement more than the air, so you have to work harder to walk. If you walked waist-deep in mud, you would have to work even harder.

Materials resist the movement of a charge in different amounts. Electrical **resistance** is the property of a material that determines how easily a charge can move through it. Electrical resistance is measured in units called **ohms.** The symbol for ohms is the Greek letter *omega* (Ω).

Most materials have some resistance. A good conductor such as copper, though, has low resistance. A good insulator, such as plastic or wood, has high resistance.

Like a thick drink in a straw, an electric charge moves more easily through a short, wide pathway than a long, narrow one.

Resistance depends on the amount and shape of the material as well as on the type of material itself. A wire that is thin has more resistance than a wire that is thick. Think of how you have to work harder to drink through a narrow straw than a wide one. A wire that is long has more resistance than a wire that is short. Again, think of how much harder it is to drink through a long straw than a short one.

CHECK YOUR READING   What three factors affect how much resistance an object has?

By taking advantage of resistance, we can use an electric charge to do work. When a moving charge overcomes resistance, some of the charge's electrical energy changes into other forms of energy, such as light and heat. For example, the filament of a light bulb is often made of tungsten, a material with high resistance. When electricity moves through the tungsten, the filament gives off light, which is useful. However, the bulb also gives off heat. Because light bulbs are not usually used to produce heat, we think of the heat they produce as wasted energy.

A three-way light bulb has two filaments, each with a different level of resistance. The one with higher resistance produces brighter light. Both together give the brightest setting.

higher resistance filament

lower resistance filament

A material with low resistance is one that a charge can flow through with little loss of energy. Materials move electricity more efficiently when they have low resistances. Such materials waste less energy, so more is available to do work at the other end. That is why copper is used for electrical wiring. Even copper has some resistance, however, and using it wastes some energy.

Superconductors

Scientists have known for many years that some materials have practically no resistance at extremely low temperatures. Such materials are called superconductors, because they conduct even better than good conductors like copper. Superconductors have many uses. They can be used in power lines to increase efficiency and conserve energy, and in high-speed trains to reduce friction. Engineers are also testing superconducting materials for use in computers and other electronic devices. Superconductors would make computers work faster and might also be used to make better motors and generators.

Because superconductors must be kept extremely cold, they have not always been practical. Scientists are solving this problem by developing superconductors that will work at higher temperatures.

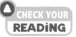 **CHECK YOUR READING** How much resistance does a superconducting material have?

Grounding

If a charge can pass through two different materials, it will pass through the one with the lower resistance. This is the principle behind an important electrical safety procedure—grounding. **Grounding** means providing a harmless, low-resistance path—a ground—for electricity to follow. In many cases, this path actually leads into the ground, that is, into the Earth.

Grounding is used to protect buildings from damage by lightning. Most buildings have some type of lightning rod, which is made from a material that is a good conductor. The rod is placed high up, so that it is closer to the lightning charge. The rod is connected to a conductor cable, and the cable is attached to a copper pole, which is driven into the ground.

Because of the rod's low resistance, lightning will strike the rod before it will strike the roof, where it might have caused a fire. Lightning hits the rod and passes harmlessly through the cable into the ground.

Grounding provides a path for electric current to travel into the ground, which can absorb the charge and make it harmless. The charge soon spreads out so that its voltage in any particular spot is low.

1. Lightning strikes the lightning rod, because the rod is the path of least resistance.

2. The rod conducts the charge to a conductor cable, which has low resistance.

3. The ground wire conducts the charge into the ground, where it spreads out and becomes harmless.

 CHECK YOUR READING   What is a ground cable?

1.2 Review

KEY CONCEPTS

1. Explain what happens when you get a static electric shock as you touch a doorknob.
2. What is electric potential?
3. What three factors affect how much electrical resistance an object has?
4. How can a lightning rod protect a building from fire?

CRITICAL THINKING

5. **Infer** Object A has a positive charge. After Object A touches Object B, A still has a positive charge and the same amount of charge. What can you infer about the charge of B?
6. **Analyze** Why do lightning rods work better if they are placed high up, closer to the lightning charge?

⬤ CHALLENGE

7. **Apply** Could the same material be used as both a conductor and an insulator? Explain your answer.

CHAPTER INVESTIGATION

Lightning

OVERVIEW AND PURPOSE Lightning is a form of static discharge. During storms, electric charges build up within clouds. Lightning occurs when these charges move. In this experiment, you will

- model the buildup of charges that can occur during a storm
- model a lightning strike
- use a ground to control the path of discharge

▶ Procedure

1. Draw a data table like the one on the sample notebook page.

2. Firmly press a lump of clay onto the inside bottom of one aluminum pan (A) to make a handle. Press another lump onto the underside of the other pan (B) as shown.

step 2

3. Place the foam plate upside down on a flat surface. Without touching the plate with your bare skin, rub the bottom of the plate vigorously with the wool cloth for 1–2 minutes.

step 3

4. Pick up aluminum pan A by the handle and hold it about 5 cm above the foam plate. Drop the pan so that it rests centered on top of the foam plate as shown. Be careful not to touch the pan or the plate.

5. Make the room as dark as possible. Slowly lower aluminum pan B over the rim of the first pan until they touch. Describe what occurs and where, in your notebook.

step 4

step 5

MATERIALS
- modeling clay
- 2 aluminum pie pans
- foam plate
- wool cloth
- paper clip

6 Repeat steps 3–5 two more times, recording your observations in your notebook.

7 Open the paper clip partway, as shown. Repeat steps 3–4. Then, instead of using the second aluminum pan, slowly bring the pointed end of the paper clip toward the rim of the first pan until they touch. Record your observations.

step 7

8 Repeat step 7 two more times, touching the paper clip to the aluminum pan in different places.

▶ Observe and Analyze | Write It Up

1. **RECORD OBSERVATIONS** Be sure your data table is complete. Draw pictures to show how the procedure varied between steps 5–6 and steps 7–8.

2. **ANALYZE** What did you observe in step 5 when the two aluminum pans touched? What do you think caused this to occur?

3. **COMPARE** How were your observations when you touched the aluminum pan with the paper clip different from those you made when you touched it with the other pan? How can you explain the difference?

▶ Conclude | Write It Up

1. **ANALYZE** Use the observations recorded in your data table to answer the following question: When you used the paper clip, why were you able to control the point at which the static discharge occurred?

2. **INFER** What charges did the foam plate and aluminum pan have before you began the experiment? after you dropped the pan on the plate? after you touched the pan with the paper clip?

3. **IDENTIFY VARIABLES** What variables and controls affected the outcome of your experiment?

4. **IDENTIFY LIMITS** What limitations or sources of error could have affected your results?

5. **APPLY** In your experiment, what corresponds to storm clouds and lightning? How did the paper clip work like a lightning rod?

▶ INVESTIGATE Further

CHALLENGE Where did the charge go when you touched the pie pan with the paper clip? Write a hypothesis to explain what happens in this situation and design an experiment to test your hypothesis.

Lightning
Observe and Analyze
Table 1. Observations of Static Discharge

Trial	Observations
With second aluminum pan	
1	
2	
3	
With paper clip	
4	
5	
6	

Conclude

1.3 Electric current is a flow of charge.

◄ **BEFORE**, you learned

- Charges move from higher to lower potential
- Materials can act as conductors or insulators
- Materials have different levels of resistance

▶ **NOW**, you will learn

- About electric current
- How current is related to voltage and resistance
- About different types of electric power cells

VOCABULARY

electric current p. 28
ampere p. 29
Ohm's law p. 29
electric cell p. 31

EXPLORE Current

How does resistance affect the flow of charge?

PROCEDURE

(1) Tape the pencil lead flat on the posterboard.

(2) Connect the wires, cell, bulb, and bulb holder as shown in the photograph.

(3) Hold the wire ends against the pencil lead about a centimeter apart from each other. Observe the bulb.

(4) Keeping the wire ends in contact with the lead, slowly move them apart. As you move the wire ends apart, observe the bulb.

WHAT DO YOU THINK?

- What happened to the bulb as you moved the wire ends apart?
- How might you explain your observation?

MATERIALS

- pencil lead
- posterboard
- electrical tape
- 3 lengths of wire
- D cell battery
- flashlight bulb
- bulb holder

Electric charge can flow continuously.

Static charges cannot make your television play. For that you need a different type of electricity. You have learned that a static charge contains a specific, limited amount of charge. You have also learned that a static charge can move and always moves from higher to lower potential. However, suppose that, instead of one charge, an electrical pathway received a continuous supply of charge and the difference in potential between the two ends of the pathway stayed the same. Then, you would have a continuous flow of charge. Another name for a flow of charge is **electric current**. Electric current is the form of electricity used to supply energy in homes, schools, and other buildings.

VOCABULARY
Don't forget to make a four square diagram for the term *electric current*.

Current, Voltage, and Resistance

Electric current obeys the same rules as moving static charges. Charge can flow only if it has a path to follow, that is, a material to conduct it. Also, charge can flow only from a point of higher potential to one of lower potential. However, one concept that does not apply to a moving static charge applies to current. Charge that flows steadily has a certain rate of flow. This rate can be measured. The standard unit of measure for current is the **ampere,** or amp. An amp is the amount of charge that flows past a given point per unit of time. One amp equals one coulomb per second. The number of amps—or amperage—of a flowing charge is determined by both voltage and resistance.

Electric current, or amperage, can be compared to the flow of water through a pipe. Electric potential, or voltage, is like pressure pushing the water through the pipe. Resistance, or ohms, is like the diameter of the pipe, which controls how much water can flow through. Water pressure and pipe size together determine the rate of water flow. Similarly, voltage and resistance together determine the rate of flow of electric charge.

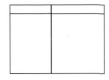

COMBINATION NOTES
In your notes, try making a sketch to help you remember how current, voltage, and resistance differ.

How Potential Affects Current

Current increases with potential, just as water flow increases with water pressure.

low pressure and low rate of flow   high pressure and high rate of flow

How Resistance Affects Current

Current decreases as resistance increases, just as water flow decreases as resistance to flow increases.

low resistance and high rate of flow   high resistance and low rate of flow

Ohm's Law

You now have three important measurements for the study of electricity: volts, ohms, and amps. The scientist for whom the ohm is named discovered a mathematical relationship among these three measurements. The relationship, called **Ohm's law,** is expressed in the formula below.

SIMULATION
CLASSZONE.COM

See Ohm's law in action.

$$\text{Current} = \frac{\text{Voltage}}{\text{Resistance}} \qquad I = \frac{V}{R}$$

I is current measured in amps (A), V is voltage measured in volts (V), and R is resistance measured in ohms (Ω).

CHECK YOUR READING   What two values do you need to know to calculate the amperage of electric current?

You have read that current is affected by both voltage and resistance. Using Ohm's law, you can calculate exactly how much it is affected and determine the exact amount of current in amps. Use the formula for current to solve the sample problem below.

Calculating Current

Sample Problem

What is the current in an electrical pathway with an electric potential of 120 volts and a resistance of 60 ohms?

What do you know?	voltage = 120 V, resistance = 60 Ω
What do you want to find out?	current
Write the formula:	$I = \dfrac{V}{R}$
Substitute into the formula:	$I = \dfrac{120 \text{ V}}{60 \text{ }\Omega}$
Calculate and simplify:	$I = 2$ A
Check that your units agree:	Unit is amps. Unit of current is amps. Units agree.
Answer:	2 A

Practice the Math

1. What is the current in an electrical pathway in which the voltage is 220 V and the resistance is 55 Ω?
2. An electrical pathway has a voltage of 12 volts and a resistance of 24 ohms. What is the current?

READING TiP

The terms *voltmeter*, *ohmmeter*, *ammeter*, and *multimeter* are all made by adding a prefix to the word *meter*.

Measuring Electricity

Volts, ohms, and amps can all be measured using specific electrical instruments. Volts can be measured with a voltmeter. Ohms can be measured with an ohmmeter. Amps can be measured with an ammeter. These three instruments are often combined in a single electrical instrument called a multimeter.

To use a multimeter, set the dial on the type of unit you wish to measure. For example, the multimeter in the photograph is being used to test the voltage of a 9-volt battery. The dial is set on volts in the 0–20 range. The meter shows that the battery's charge has an electric potential of more than 9 volts, which means that the battery is good. A dead battery would have a lower voltage.

CHECK YOUR READING   What does an ohmmeter measure?

How can you produce electric current?

PROCEDURE

1. Insert the paper clip and the penny into the lemon, as shown in the photograph. The penny and paper clip should go about 3 cm into the lemon. They should be close, but not touching.

2. On the multimeter, go to the DC volts (V===) section of the dial and select the 0–2000 millivolt range (2000 m).

3. Touch one of the leads of the multimeter to the paper clip. Touch the other lead to the penny. Observe what is shown on the display of the multimeter.

WHAT DO YOU THINK?

- What did you observe on the display of the multimeter?
- How can you explain the reading on the multimeter?

CHALLENGE Repeat this experiment using different combinations of fruits or vegetables and metal objects. Which combinations work best?

MATERIALS
- paper clip
- penny
- large lemon
- multimeter
For Challenge
- additional fruits or vegetables
- metal objects

TIME
20 minutes

Electric cells supply electric current.

Electric current can be used in many ways. Two basic types of device have been developed for producing current. One type produces electric current using magnets. You will learn more about this technology in Chapter 3. The other type is the **electric cell,** which produces electric current using the chemical or physical properties of different materials.

Electrochemical Cells

An electrochemical cell is an electric cell that produces current by means of chemical reactions. As you can see in the diagram, an electrochemical cell contains two strips made of different materials. The strips are called electrodes. The electrodes are suspended in a third material called the electrolyte, which interacts chemically with the electrodes to separate charges and produce a flow of electrons from the negative terminal to the positive terminal.

Batteries are made using electrochemical cells. Technically, a battery is two or more cells connected to each other. However, single cells, such as C cells and D cells, are often referred to as batteries.

flow of electrons

positive terminal

negative terminal

electrode

electrolyte

electrode

Primary Cells The electrochemical cell shown on page 31 is called a wet cell, because the electrolyte is a liquid. Most household batteries in use today have a solid paste electrolyte and so are called dry cells. Both wet cells and dry cells are primary cells. Primary cells produce electric current through chemical reactions that continue until one or more of the chemicals is used up.

The primary cell on page 33 is a typical zinc-carbon dry cell. It has a negative electrode made of zinc. The zinc electrode is made in the shape of a can and has a terminal—in this case, a wide disk of exposed metal—on the bottom of the cell. The positive electrode consists of a carbon rod and particles of carbon and manganese dioxide. The particles are suspended in an electrolyte paste. The positive electrode has a terminal—a smaller disk of exposed metal—at the top of the rod. A paper separator prevents the two electrodes from coming into contact inside the cell.

When the two terminals of the cell are connected—for example, when you turn on a flashlight—a chemical reaction between the zinc and the electrolyte produces electrons and positive zinc ions. The electrons flow through the wires connecting the cell to the flashlight bulb, causing the bulb to light up. The electrons then travel through the carbon rod and combine with the manganese dioxide. When the zinc and manganese dioxide stop reacting, the cell dies.

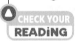 **CHECK YOUR READING** Why are most household batteries called dry cells?

Storage Cells Some batteries produce current through chemical reactions that can be reversed inside the battery. These batteries are called storage cells, secondary cells, or rechargeable batteries. A car battery like the lead-acid battery shown on page 33 is rechargeable. The battery has a negative electrode of lead and a positive electrode of lead peroxide. As the battery produces current, both electrodes change chemically into lead sulfate, and the electrolyte changes into water.

When storage cells are producing current, they are said to be discharging. Whenever a car engine is started, the battery discharges to operate the ignition motor. A car's battery can also be used when the car is not running to operate the lights or other appliances. If the battery is used too long in discharge mode, it will run down completely.

While a car is running, however, the battery is continually being charged. A device called an alternator, which is run by the car's engine, produces current. When electrons flow into the battery in the reverse direction from discharging, the chemical reactions that produce current are reversed. The ability of the battery to produce current is renewed.

 CHECK YOUR READING What kind of battery can be charged by reversing chemical reactions?

Batteries

Both primary cells and storage cells produce electricity through chemical reactions.

Flashlights use **primary cells.**

Car batteries and cell phones use **storage cells.**

Primary Cell

Primary cells produce electric current through chemical reactions. The reactions continue until the chemicals are used up.

flow of electrons

terminal

separator

+

zinc can

carbon rod

terminal

−

manganese dioxide particles in paste electrolyte

Storage Cell

① **Discharging** Storage cells produce current through chemical reactions that can be reversed in the battery.

alternator

flow of electrons

lead sulfate

mostly water

starter motor

② **Charging** Sending current through the battery in the opposite direction reverses the chemical reactions.

lead peroxide (blue)

lead (red)

mostly sulfuric acid

READING VISUALS In which direction do electrons flow when a storage cell is being charged?

The word *solar* comes from the Latin word *sol,* which means the Sun.

Solar Cells

Some materials, such as silicon, can absorb energy from the Sun or other sources of light and then give off electrons, producing electric current. Electric cells made from such materials are called solar cells.

Solar cells are often used to make streetlights come on automatically at night. Current from the cell operates a switch that keeps the lights turned off. When it gets dark, the current stops, the switch closes, and the streetlights come on.

This NASA research aircraft is powered only by the solar cells on its upper surface.

Many houses and other buildings now get at least some of their power from solar cells. Sunlight provides an unlimited source of free, environmentally safe energy. However, it is not always easy or cheap to use that energy. It must be collected and stored because solar cells do not work at night or when sunlight is blocked by clouds or buildings.

 CHECK YOUR READING Where do solar cells get their energy?

1.3 Review

KEY CONCEPTS

1. How is electric current different from a static charge that moves?

2. How can Ohm's law be used to calculate the electrical resistance of a piece of wire?

3. How do rechargeable batteries work differently from nonrechargeable ones?

CRITICAL THINKING

4. **Infer** Electrical outlets in a house maintain a steady voltage, even when the amount of resistance on them changes. How is this possible?

5. **Analyze** Why don't solar cells eventually run down as electrochemical cells do?

CHALLENGE

6. **Apply** Several kinds of electric cells are discussed in this section. Which do you think would be the most practical source of electrical energy on a long trek through the desert? Explain your reasoning.

MATH in SCIENCE

MATH TUTORIAL
CLASSZONE.COM

Click on Math Tutorial for more help with equations.

Which Formula Is Best?

A rock band needs an amplifier, and an amplifier needs a volume control. A volume control works by controlling the amount of resistance in an electrical pathway. When resistance goes down, the current—and the volume—go up. Ohm's law expresses the relationship among voltage (V), resistance (R), and amperage (I). If you know the values of two variables, you can use Ohm's law to find the third. The law can be written in three ways, depending on which variable you wish to find.

$$I = \frac{V}{R} \qquad R = \frac{V}{I} \qquad V = IR$$

A simple way to remember these three versions of the formula is to use the pyramid diagram below. Cover up the variable you are looking for. The visible part of the diagram will give you the correct formula to use.

Example

What is the voltage of a battery that produces a current of 1 amp through a wire with a resistance of 9 ohms?

(1) You want to find voltage, so cover up the V in the pyramid diagram. To find V, the correct formula to use is V = IR.

(2) Insert the known values into the formula. V = 1 A • 9 Ω

(3) Solve the equation to find the missing variable. 1 • 9 = 9

ANSWER 9 volts

Answer the following questions.

1. What is the voltage of a battery that sends 3 amps of current through a wire with a resistance of 4 ohms?

2. What is the resistance of a wire in which the current is 2 amps if the battery producing the current has a voltage of 220 volts?

3. What is the amperage of a current at 120 volts through a wire with a resistance of 5 ohms?

CHALLENGE Dimmer switches also work by varying resistance. A club owner likes the way the lights look at 1/3 normal current. The normal current is 15 amps. The voltage is constant at 110 V. How much resistance will he need?

A volume control works by changing the amount of resistance to the flow of current.

Chapter Review

the **BIG** idea

Moving electric charges transfer energy.

 CONTENT REVIEW
CLASSZONE.COM

◀ KEY CONCEPTS SUMMARY

1.1 Materials can become electrically charged.

Electric charge is a property of matter.

| Electrons have a negative charge. | Protons have a positive charge. | Unlike charges attract. | Like charges repel. |

Static charges are caused by the movement of electrons, resulting in an imbalance of positive and negative charges.

VOCABULARY
electric charge p. 10
electric field p. 10
static charge p. 11
induction p. 13

1.2 Charges can move from one place to another.

Charge movement is affected by
• electric potential, measured in volts
• resistance, measured in ohms

A conductor has low resistance.

An insulator has high resistance.

A ground is the path of least resistance.

VOCABULARY
electric potential p. 19
volt p. 19
conductor p. 22
insulator p. 22
resistance p. 23
ohm p. 23
grounding p. 25

1.3 Electric current is a flow of charge.

Electric current is measured in amperes, or amps.

Ohm's law states that current equals voltage divided by resistance.

Electrochemical cells produce electric current through chemical reactions.

VOCABULARY
electric current p. 28
ampere p. 29
Ohm's law p. 29
electric cell p. 31

Reviewing Vocabulary

Copy the chart below, and write each term's definition. Use the meanings of the underlined roots to help you.

Word	Root	Definition
EXAMPLE current	to run	continuous flow of charge
1. static charge	standing	
2. induction	into + to lead	
3. electric cell	chamber	
4. conductor	with + to lead	
5. insulator	island	
6. resistance	to stop	
7. electric potential	power	
8. grounding	surface of Earth	

Write a vocabulary term to match each clue.

9. In honor of scientist Alessandro Volta (1745–1827)

10. In honor of the scientist who discovered the relationship among voltage, resistance, and current

11. The amount of charge that flows past a given point in a unit of time.

Reviewing Key Concepts

Multiple Choice *Choose the letter of the best answer.*

12. An electric charge is a
 a. kind of liquid
 b. reversible chemical reaction
 c. type of matter
 d. force acting at a distance

13. A static charge is different from electric current in that a static charge
 a. never moves
 b. can either move or not move
 c. moves only when resistance is low enough
 d. moves only when voltage is high enough

14. Charging by induction means charging
 a. with battery power
 b. by direct contact
 c. at a distance
 d. using solar power

15. Electric potential describes
 a. the electric potential energy per unit charge
 b. the electric kinetic energy per unit charge
 c. whether an electric charge is positive or negative
 d. how an electric charge is affected by gravity

16. A superconductor is a material that, when very cold, has no
 a. amperage
 b. resistance
 c. electric charge
 d. electric potential

17. Ohm's law says that when resistance goes up, current
 a. increases   **c.** stays the same
 b. decreases   **d.** matches voltage

18. Electrochemical cells include
 a. all materials that build up a charge
 b. primary cells and storage cells
 c. batteries and solar cells
 d. storage cells and lightning rods

Short Answer *Write a short answer to each question.*

19. What determines whether a charge you get when walking across a rug is positive or negative?

20. What is the difference between resistance and insulation?

21. What is one disadvantage of solar cells?

Use the diagram of an electrochemical cell below to answer the next three questions.

22. ANALYZE In which direction do electrons flow between the two terminals?

23. PREDICT What changes will occur in the cell as it discharges?

24. ANALYZE What determines whether the cell is rechargeable or not?

Use the graph below to answer the next three questions.

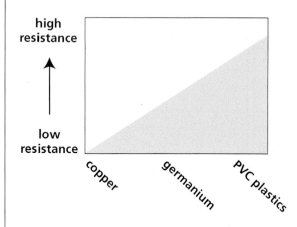

25. INFER Which material could you probably use as an insulator?

26. INFER Which material could be used in a lightning rod?

27. APPLY Materials that conduct electrons under some—but not all—conditions are known as semiconductors. Which material is probably a semiconductor?

Use the formula for Ohm's law to answer the next four questions.

$$I = \frac{V}{R}$$

28. An electrical pathway has a voltage of 240 volts and a current of 10 amperes. What is the resistance?

29. A 240-volt air conditioner has a resistance of 8 ohms. What is the current?

30. An electrical pathway has a current of 1.2 amperes and resistance of 40 ohms. What is the voltage?

31. An electrical pathway has a voltage of 400 volts and resistance of 2000 ohms. What is the current?

the BIG idea

32. INFER Look back at the photograph on pages 6 and 7. Based on what you have learned in this chapter, describe what you think is happening to keep the dragon lit.

33. COMPARE AND CONTRAST Draw two simple diagrams to compare and contrast static charges and electric current. Add labels and captions to make your comparison clear. Then write a paragraph summarizing the comparison.

UNIT PROJECTS

If you are doing a unit project, make a folder for your project. Include in your folder a list of the resources you will need, the date on which the project is due, and a schedule to keep track of your progress. Begin gathering data.

Interpreting Diagrams

Use the illustration below to answer the following questions. Assume that the balloons start off with no net charge.

1. What will happen if a negatively charged rod is brought near one of the balloons without touching it?

   a. The balloons will move toward each other.

   b. The balloons will move away from each other.

   c. Electrons on the balloons will move toward the rod.

   d. Electrons on the balloons will move away from the rod.

2. What will happen if a positively charged rod is brought near one of the balloons without touching it?

   a. The balloons will move toward each other.

   b. The balloons will move away from each other.

   c. Electrons on the balloons will move toward the rod.

   d. Electrons on the balloons will move away from the rod.

3. In the previous question, the effect of the rod on the balloons is an example of

   a. charging by contact   **c.** induction

   b. charge polarization   **d.** conduction

4. What will happen if a negatively charged rod is brought near one of the balloons and the balloons are then separated?

   a. The balloon farthest from the rod will become positively charged.

   b. The balloon farthest from the rod will become negatively charged.

   c. Both balloons will become positively charged.

   d. Both balloons will have no net charge.

5. If you rub one balloon in your hair to charge it and then move it close to the other balloon, the balloons will

   a. not move

   b. move away from each other

   c. move toward the ground

   d. move toward each other

6. What will happen if a negatively charged rod is brought near one of the balloons, then taken away, and the balloons are then separated?

   a. The balloon farthest from the rod will become positively charged.

   b. The balloon farthest from the rod will become negatively charged.

   c. Both balloons will become positively charged.

   d. Both balloons will have no net charge.

Extended Response

Answer the two questions below in detail. Include some of the terms from the word box. Underline each term that you use in your answers.

| charge separation   recharging   resistance |
| source of current   static charge   induce |

7. Describe the events leading up to and including a bolt of lightning striking Earth from a storm cloud.

8. Explain the advantages and disadvantages of storage cells over other types of electric cells.

2 Circuits and Electronics

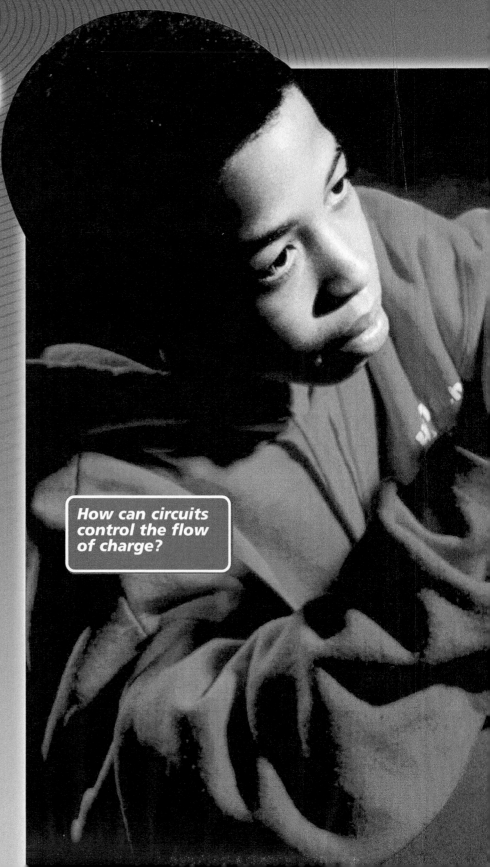

the **BIG** idea

Circuits control the flow of electric charge.

Key Concepts

SECTION

2.1 **Charge needs a continuous path to flow.**
Learn how circuits are used to control the flow of charge.

SECTION

2.2 **Circuits make electric current useful.**
Learn about series circuits and parallel circuits.

SECTION

2.3 **Electronic technology is based on circuits.**
Learn about computers and other electronic devices.

How can circuits control the flow of charge?

Internet Preview

CLASSZONE.COM

Chapter 2 online resources: Content Review, Simulation, Visualization, two Resource Centers, Math Tutorial, Test Practice

EXPLORE (the BIG idea)

Will the Flashlight Still Work?

Experiment with a flashlight to find out if it will work in any of the following arrangements: with one of the batteries facing the wrong way, with a piece of paper between the batteries, or with one battery removed. In each case, switch on the flashlight and observe.

Observe and Think
When did the flashlight work? Why do you think it worked or did not work in each case?

What's Inside a Calculator?

Use a small screwdriver to open a simple calculator. Look at the circuit board inside.

Observe and Think How do you think the metal lines relate to the buttons on the front of the calculator? to the display? What is the source of electrical energy? How is it connected to the rest of the circuit?

Internet Activity: Circuits

Go to **ClassZone.com** to build a virtual circuit. See if you can complete the circuit and light the bulb.

Observe and Think
What parts are necessary to light the bulb? What happened when you opened the switch? closed the switch?

Electronic Circuits **Code: MDL066**

Getting Ready to Learn

◀ CONCEPT REVIEW

- Energy can change from one form to another.
- Energy can move from one place to another.
- Current is the flow of charge through a conductor.

◀ VOCABULARY REVIEW

electric current p. 28
electric potential p. 18
conductor p. 22
resistance p. 23
ampere p. 29

ⓘ CONTENT REVIEW
CLASSZONE.COM
Review concepts and vocabulary.

▶ TAKING NOTES

OUTLINE

As you read, copy the headings on your paper in the form of an outline. Then add notes in your own words that summarize what you read.

VOCABULARY STRATEGY

Write each new vocabulary term in the center of a **frame game** diagram. Decide what information to frame it with. Use examples, descriptions, parts, sentences that use the term in context, or pictures. You can change the frame to fit each term.

See the Note-Taking Handbook on pages R45–R51.

SCIENCE NOTEBOOK

I. ELECTRIC CHARGE FLOWS IN A LOOP.
   A. THE PARTS OF A CIRCUIT
      1. voltage source
      2. connection
      3. electrical device
      4. switch

Electrical device

Part of a circuit | RESISTOR | Light bulb is an example

Slows the flow of charge

Charge needs a continuous path to flow.

 BEFORE, you learned

- Current is the flow of charge
- Voltage is a measure of electric potential
- Materials affect the movement of charge

 NOW, you will learn

- About the parts of a circuit
- How a circuit functions
- How safety devices stop current

VOCABULARY

circuit p. 43
resistor p. 44
short circuit p. 46

EXPLORE Circuits

How can you light the bulb?

PROCEDURE

1. Tape one end of a strip of foil to the negative terminal, or the flat end, of the battery. Tape the other end of the foil to the tip at the base of the light bulb, as shown.

2. Tape the second strip of foil to the positive terminal, or the raised end, of the battery.

3. Find a way to make the bulb light.

WHAT DO YOU THINK?
- How did you make the bulb light?
- Can you find other arrangements that make the bulb light?

MATERIALS
- 2 strips of aluminum foil
- electrical tape
- D cell (battery)
- light bulb

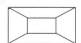

VOCABULARY
Use a frame game diagram to record the term *circuit* in your notebook.

Electric charge flows in a loop.

In the last chapter, you read that current is electric charge that flows from one place to another. Charge does not flow continuously through a material unless the material forms a closed path, or loop. A **circuit** is a closed path through which a continuous charge can flow. The path is provided by a low-resistance material, or conductor, usually wire. Circuits are designed to do specific jobs, such as light a bulb.

Circuits can be found all around you and serve many different purposes. In this chapter, you will read about simple circuits, such as the ones in flashlights, and more complex circuits, such as the ones that run toys, cameras, computers, and more.

 CHECK YOUR READING How are circuits related to current?

The Parts of a Circuit

The illustration below shows a simple circuit. Circuits typically contain the following parts. Some circuits contain many of each part.

REMINDER

Remember, a battery consists of two or more cells.

1 Voltage Source The voltage source in a circuit provides the electric potential for charge to flow through the circuit. Batteries are often the voltage sources in a circuit. A power plant may also be a voltage source. When you plug an appliance into an outlet, a circuit is formed that goes all the way to a power plant and back.

2 Conductor A circuit must be a closed path in order for charge to flow. That means that there must be a conductor, such as wire, that forms a connection from the voltage source to the electrical device and back.

3 Switch A switch is a part of a circuit designed to break the closed path of charge. When a switch is open, it produces a gap in the circuit so that the charge cannot flow.

4 Electrical Device An electrical device is any part of the circuit that changes electrical energy into another form of energy. A **resistor** is an electrical device that slows the flow of charge in a circuit. When the charge is slowed, some energy is converted to light or heat. A light bulb is an example of a resistor.

Circuit Parts

The parts of a basic circuit include a voltage source, conductor, switch, and one or more electrical devices.

3 A **switch** is used to open and close the circuit.

2 The **conductor** provides a path through which charge can flow.

1 The **voltage source** supplies electrical energy to the circuit.

4 The resistor is an **electrical device** that converts electrical energy into another form of energy.

READING VISUALS Would the light bulb be lit if there were no switch in this circuit? Why or why not?

Open and Closed Circuits

Current in a circuit is similar to water running through a hose. The flow of charge differs from the flow of water in an important way, however. The water does not require a closed path to flow. If you cut the hose, the water continues to flow. If you cut a wire, the charge stops flowing.

Batteries have connections at both ends so that charge can follow a closed path to and from the battery. The cords that you see on appliances might look like single cords but actually contain at least two wires. The wires connect the device to a power plant and back to make a closed path.

Switches work by opening and closing the circuit. A switch that is on closes the circuit and allows charge to flow through the electrical devices. A switch that is off opens the circuit and stops the current.

REMINDER

Current requires a closed loop.

CHECK YOUR READING How are switches used to control the flow of charge through a circuit?

Standard symbols are used to represent the parts of a circuit. Some common symbols are shown in the circuit diagrams below. The diagrams represent the circuit shown on page 44 with the switch in both open and closed positions. Electricians and architects use diagrams such as these to plan the wiring of a building.

Circuit Diagrams

Symbols are used to represent the parts of a circuit. The circuit diagrams below show the circuit from page 44 in both an open and closed position.

READING VISUALS Would charge flow through the circuit diagrammed on the left? Why or why not?

Current follows the path of least resistance.

OUTLINE

Add this heading to your outline, along with supporting ideas.

I. Main idea
  A. Supporting idea
    1. Detail
    2. Detail
  B. Supporting idea

Since current can follow only a closed path, why are damaged cords so dangerous? And why are people warned to stay away from fallen power lines? Although current follows a closed path, the path does not have to be made of wire. A person can become a part of the circuit, too. Charge flowing through a person is dangerous and sometimes deadly.

Current follows the path of least resistance. Materials with low resistance, such as certain metals, are good conductors. Charge will flow through a copper wire but not the plastic coating that covers it because copper is a good conductor and plastic is not. Water is also a good conductor when mixed with salt from a person's skin. That is why it is dangerous to use electrical devices near water.

Short Circuits

A **short circuit** is an unintended path connecting one part of a circuit with another. The current in a short circuit follows a closed path, but the path is not the one it was intended to follow. The illustration below shows a functioning circuit and a short circuit.

1 **Functioning Circuit** The charge flows through one wire, through the light bulb, and then back through the second wire to the outlet.

2 **Short Circuit** The cord has been damaged and the two wires inside have formed a connection. Now the path of least resistance is through one wire and back through the second wire.

coating

wires

In the second case, without the resistance from the lamp, there is more current in the wires. Too much current can overheat the wires and start a fire. When a power line falls, charge flows along the wire and into the ground. If someone touches that power line, the person's body becomes part of the path of charge. That much charge flowing through a human body is almost always deadly.

RESOURCE CENTER
CLASSZONE.COM

Explore resources on electrical safety.

 CHECK YOUR READING Why are short circuits dangerous?

Grounding a Circuit

Recall that when lightning strikes a lightning rod, charge flows into the ground through a highly conductive metal rod rather than through a person or a building. In other words, the current follows the path of least resistance. The third prong on some electrical plugs performs a similar function. A circuit that connects stray current safely to the ground is known as a grounded circuit. Because the third prong grounds the circuit, it is sometimes called the ground.

SAFETY TIPS

- Never go near a fallen power line.

- Never touch an electrical appliance when you are in the shower or bathtub.

- Always dry your hands thoroughly before using an electrical appliance.

- Never use an electrical cord that is damaged in any way.

- Never bend or cut a ground prong in order to make a grounded plug fit into an ungrounded outlet.

In this illustration, green represents the path that connects the appliance and the outlet to the ground.

Orange is used in this illustration to represent the path that connects the appliance's circuit to a power source and back.

ground wire

connects to ground wire

Normally, charge flows through one prong, along a wire to an appliance, then back along a second wire to the second prong. If there is a short circuit, the charge might flow dangerously to the outside of the shell of the appliance. If there is a ground wire, the current will flow along the third wire and safely into the ground, along either a buried rod or a cold water pipe.

 What is the purpose of a ground wire?

Safety devices control current.

Suppose your living room wiring consists of a circuit that supplies current to a television and several lights. One hot evening, you turn on an air conditioner in the living room window. The wires that supply current to the room are suddenly carrying more current than before. The lights in the room become dim. Too much current in a circuit is dangerous. How do you know if there is too much current in a wire?

Fortunately, people have been using electric current for over a hundred years. An understanding of how charge flows has led to the development of safety devices. These safety devices are built into circuits to prevent dangerous situations from occurring.

How Fuses Work

new
fuse

blown
fuse

If you turn on an air conditioner in a room full of other electrical appliances that are already on, the circuit could overheat. But if the circuit contains a fuse, the fuse will automatically shut off the current. A fuse is a safety device that opens a circuit when there is too much current in it. Fuses are typically found in older homes and buildings. They are also found in cars and electrical appliances like air conditioners.

A fuse consists of a thin strip of metal that is inserted into the circuit. The charge in the closed circuit flows through the fuse. If too much charge flows through the fuse, the metal strip melts. When the strip has melted and the circuit is open, the fuse is blown. The photographs on the left show a new fuse and a blown fuse. As you can see, charge cannot flow across the melted strip. It has broken the circuit and stopped the current.

How much current is too much? That varies. The electrician who installs a circuit knows how much current the wiring can handle. He or she uses that knowledge to choose the right kind of fuse. Fuses are measured in amperes, or amps. Remember that amperage is a measure of current. If a fuse has blown, it must be replaced with a fuse of the same amperage. But a fuse should be replaced only after the problem that caused it to blow has been fixed.

Other Safety Devices

Most modern homes do not use fuses. Instead, they use safety devices called circuit breakers. Circuit breakers, unlike fuses, do not have to be replaced every time they open the circuit. Like fuses, circuit breakers automatically open the circuit when too much charge flows through it. If the circuit becomes overloaded or there is a short circuit, the wire and the breaker grow hot. That makes a piece of metal inside the breaker expand. As it expands, it presses against a switch. The switch is then flipped to the off position and the current is stopped. Once the problem is solved, power can be restored manually by simply flipping the switch back. The illustration on the right shows a circuit breaker.

open circuit

circuit breaker

 How are circuit breakers similar to fuses?

The photograph at the bottom right shows another safety device—a ground-fault circuit interrupter (GFCI) outlet. Sometimes a little current leaks out of an outlet or an appliance. Often it is so small you do not notice it. But if you happen to have wet hands, touching even a small current can be very dangerous.

GFCI outlets are required in places where exposure to water is common, such as in kitchens and bathrooms. A tiny circuit inside the GFCI outlet monitors the current going out and coming in. If some of the current starts to flow through an unintended path, there will be less current coming in to the GFCI. If that happens, a circuit breaker inside the GFCI outlet opens the circuit and stops the current. To close the circuit again, you push "Reset."

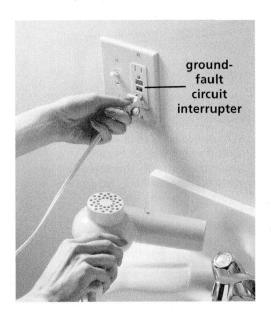

ground-fault circuit interrupter

2.1 Review

KEY CONCEPTS

1. Describe three parts of a circuit and explain what each part does.
2. Explain the function of a ground wire.
3. What do fuses and circuit breakers have in common?

CRITICAL THINKING

4. **Apply** Suppose you have built a circuit for a class project. You are using a flat piece of wood for its base. How could you make a switch out of a paperclip and two nails?
5. **Communicate** Draw a diagram of a short circuit. Use the symbols for the parts of a circuit.

CHALLENGE

6. **Evaluate** A fuse in a home has blown and the owner wants to replace it with a fuse that can carry more current. Why might the owner's decision lead to a dangerous situation?

ELECTRICIAN

The Science of Electrical Work

Electricians are the professionals who know how to control and modify electrical installations safely. They are the people who install the wiring and fixtures that deliver current to the appliances in your home. They also inspect equipment and wiring to locate and correct problems. High-voltage current can cause injuries, or even death, if not handled correctly. The electrician uses science to build and repair electrical systems safely.

Choosing the Wire

Different types and thicknesses of wire have different amounts of resistance and can carry different amounts of current without overheating. The electrician knows which type of wire is suitable for each application.

Installing Safety Devices

Circuit breakers shut off a circuit when the wires carry too much current. This safety device protects the wires from overheating. The electrician chooses circuit breakers with the appropriate amperage for each circuit.

Using Circuit Diagrams

Circuit diagrams are used to map all of the circuits in a project. The electrician determines how many electrical devices each one will contain and knows how much energy those devices will use.

EXPLORE

1. **INFER** Look around the room you're in for electrical outlets. Why do you think each one is located where it is? Do you think they all connect appliances to the same circuit? Explain how this is possible.

2. **CHALLENGE** Suppose you are planning the wiring for the lighting in a room. Draw a diagram of the room's layout and indicate where the wires, lighting fixtures, and switches will be located.

Circuits make electric current useful.

BEFORE, you learned	NOW, you will learn
• Charge flows in a closed circuit	• How circuits are designed for specific purposes
• Circuits have a voltage source, conductor, and one or more electrical devices	• How a series circuit differs from a parallel circuit
• Current follows the path of least resistance	• How electrical appliances use circuits

VOCABULARY

series circuit p. 52
parallel circuit p. 53

THINK ABOUT

How does it work?

You know what a telephone does. But did you ever stop to think about how the circuits and other electrical parts inside of it work together to make it happen?

This photo shows an old telephone that has been taken apart to reveal its circuits. As you can see, there are a lot of different parts. Each one has a function. Pick two or three of the parts. What do you think each part does? How do you think it works? How might it relate to the other parts inside the telephone?

OUTLINE

Remember to include this heading in your outline.

I. Main idea
  A. Supporting idea
    1. Detail
    2. Detail
  B. Supporting idea

Circuits are constructed for specific purposes.

How many things around you right now use electric current? Current is used to transfer energy to so many things because it is easy to store, distribute, and turn off and on. Each device that uses current is a part of at least one circuit—the circuit that supplies its voltage.

Most electrical appliances have many circuits inside of them that are designed to carry out specific functions. Those circuits may be designed to light bulbs, move motor parts, or calculate. Each of those circuits may have thousands—or even millions—of parts. The functions that a circuit can perform depend on how those parts are set up within the circuit.

 CHECK YOUR READING Why is the design of a circuit important?

Circuits can have multiple paths.

Even a simple circuit can contain several parts. When you flip the light switch in your classroom, how many different lights go on? If you count each light bulb or each fluorescent tube, there might be as many as ten or twelve light bulbs. There is more than one way those light bulbs could be connected in one circuit. Next, you will read about two simple ways that circuits can be constructed.

Series Circuits

READING TIP

The word *series* means a number of things arranged one after another.

A **series circuit** is a circuit in which current follows a single path. That means that all of the parts in a series circuit are part of the same path. The photograph and diagram below show a series circuit. The charge coming from the D cell flows first through one light bulb, and then through the next one.

Series Circuit

Each device in a series circuit is wired on a single path.

A series circuit uses a minimal amount of wire. However, a disadvantage of a series circuit is that all of the elements must be in working order for the circuit to function. If one of the light bulbs burns out, the circuit will be broken and the other bulb will be dark, too. Series circuits have another disadvantage. Light bulbs and other resistors convert some energy into heat and light. The more light bulbs that are added to a series circuit, the less current there is available, and the dimmer all of the bulbs become.

 CHECK YOUR READING Give two disadvantages of a series circuit.

If voltage sources are arranged in series, the voltages will add together. Sometimes batteries are arranged in series to add voltage to a circuit. For example, the circuits in flashlights are usually series circuits. The charge flows through one battery, through the next, through the bulb, and back to the first battery. The flashlight is brighter than it would be if its circuit contained only a single battery.

Parallel Circuits

A **parallel circuit** is a circuit in which current follows more than one path. Each path is called a branch. The current divides among all possible branches, so that the voltage is the same across each branch. The photograph and diagram below show a simple parallel circuit.

Parallel Circuit

Each device in a parallel circuit has its own connection to the voltage source.

Parallel circuits require more wire than do series circuits. On the other hand, there is more than one path on which the charge may flow. If one bulb burns out, the other bulb will continue to glow. As you add more and more light bulbs to a series circuit, each bulb in the circuit grows dimmer and dimmer. Because each bulb you add in a parallel circuit has its own branch to the power source, the bulbs burn at their brightest.

A flashlight contains batteries wired in a series circuit. Batteries can be wired in parallel, too. If the two positive terminals are connected to each other and the two negative terminals are connected to each other, charge will flow from both batteries. Adding batteries in parallel will not increase the voltage supplied to the circuit, but the batteries will last longer.

to voltage source

Kitchen Parallel Circuit

LIGHT OUTLET MICROWAVE VOLTAGE SOURCE

The circuits in most businesses and homes are connected in parallel. Look at the illustration of the kitchen and its wiring. This is a parallel circuit, so even if one electrical device is switched off, the others can still be used. The circuits within many electrical devices are combinations of series circuits and parallel circuits. For example, a parallel circuit may have branches that contain several elements arranged in series.

 CHECK YOUR READING Why are the circuits in buildings and homes arranged in parallel?

How can you produce brighter light?

PROCEDURE

1. Clip one end of a wire to the light bulb and the other end to the negative terminal of one battery to form a connection.

2. Use another wire to connect the positive terminal of the battery with the negative terminal of a second battery, as shown in the photograph.

3. Use a third wire to connect the positive terminal of the second battery to the light bulb. Observe the light bulb.

4. Remove the wires. Find a way to reconnect the wires to produce the other type of circuit.

WHAT DO YOU THINK?

- Which circuit produced brighter light? What type of circuit was it?

- Why did the light bulb glow brighter in that circuit?

CHALLENGE Suppose you wanted to construct a new circuit consisting of four light bulbs and only one battery. How would you arrange the light bulbs so that they glow at their brightest? Your answer should be in the form of either a diagram or a sketch of the circuit.

SKILL FOCUS
Inferring

MATERIALS
- 4 insulated wires with alligator clips
- small light bulb in a holder
- 2 batteries in holders

TIME
15 minutes

Circuits convert electrical energy into other forms of energy.

We use electrical energy to do many things besides lighting a string of light bulbs. For example, a circuit in a space heater converts electrical energy into heat. A circuit in a fan converts electrical energy into motion. A circuit in a bell converts electrical energy into sound. That bell might also be on a circuit that makes it ring at certain times, letting you know when class is over.

Branches, switches, and other elements in circuits allow for such control of current that our calculators and computers can use circuits to calculate and process information for us. All of these things are possible because voltage is electric potential that can be converted into energy in a circuit.

 Name three types of energy that electrical energy can be converted into.

A toaster is an example of an electrical appliance containing a circuit that converts energy from one form to another. In a toaster, electrical energy is converted into heat. Voltage is supplied to the toaster by plugging it into a wall outlet, which completes the circuit from a power plant. The outlet is wired in parallel with other outlets, so the appliance will always be connected to the same amount of voltage.

3 spring

handle

2 heating element

1 contact points

1 When you push the handle down, a piece of metal connects to contact points on a circuit board that act as a switch and run current through the circuit.

2 Charge flows through a resistor in the circuit called a heating element. The heating element is made up of a type of wire that has a very high resistance. As charge flows through the heating element, electrical energy is converted into heat.

3 The holder in the toaster is loaded onto a timed spring. After a certain amount of time passes, the spring is released, the toast pops up, and the circuit is opened. The toaster shuts off automatically, and your toast is done.

 CHECK YOUR READING Summarize the way a circuit in a toaster works. (Remember that a summary includes only the most important information.)

2.2 Review

KEY CONCEPTS

1. Explain how a circuit can perform a specific function.

2. How are series circuits and parallel circuits similar? How do they differ?

3. Describe three electrical appliances that use circuits to convert electrical energy into other forms of energy.

CRITICAL THINKING

4. **Analyze** Why are the batteries of flashlights often arranged in series and not in parallel?

5. **Infer** You walk past a string of small lights around a window frame. Only two of the bulbs are burned out. What can you tell about the string of lights?

CHALLENGE

6. **Apply** Explain how the circuit in a space heater converts electrical energy into heat. Draw a diagram of the circuit, using the standard symbols for circuit diagrams.

MATH TUTORIAL
CLASSZONE.COM

Click on Math Tutorial for
more help with percents
and proportions.

Voltage Drop

A voltage drop occurs when current passes through a wire or an
electrical device. The higher the resistance of a wire, the greater
the voltage drop. Too much voltage drop can cause the device
to overheat.

The National Electric Code—a document of guidelines for electricians—states that the voltage drop across a wire should be no
more than 5 percent of the voltage from the voltage source. To find
5 percent of a number, you can set up the calculation as a proportion.

Example

The lighting in a hotel includes many fixtures that will be
arranged on long wires. The electrician needs to know the maximum voltage drop allowed in order to choose the proper wire.
The circuit will use a voltage source of 120 V. What is 5% of 120?

(1) Write the problem as a proportion.

$$\frac{\text{voltage drop}}{\text{voltage}} = \frac{\text{percent}}{100}$$

(2) Substitute.

$$\frac{\text{voltage drop}}{120} = \frac{5}{100}$$

(3) Calculate and simplify.

$$\frac{\text{voltage drop}}{\cancel{120}} \cdot \cancel{120} = \frac{5}{100} \cdot 120$$

$$\text{voltage drop} = 6$$

ANSWER The maximum voltage drop in the wire is 6 V.

Use the proportion to answer the following questions.

1. If the voltage source is increased to 277 V, what is the maximum
   voltage drop in the wire?

2. To be on the safe side, the electrician decided to find a wire
   with a voltage drop that is 3 percent of the voltage from the
   voltage source. What is the voltage drop in the wire?

CHALLENGE A student wants to hang a string of lights outside and connect it to an extension cord. The voltage drop
across the extension cord is 3.1 V. The outlet supplies 240 V.
Does the voltage drop in the extension cord meet the code
guidelines?

The many lights in this spectacular display
in Kobe, Japan, produce a large voltage
drop. The appropriate type of wire must
be used to supply its current.

Electronic technology is based on circuits.

◁ BEFORE, you learned

- Charge flows in a closed loop
- Circuits are designed for specific purposes
- Electrical appliances use circuits

▷ NOW, you will learn

- How information can be coded
- How computer circuits use digital information
- How computers work

VOCABULARY

electronic p. 57
binary code p. 58
digital p. 58
analog p. 60
computer p. 61

EXPLORE Codes

How can information be coded?

PROCEDURE

(1) Write the numbers 1 to 26 in your notebook. Below each number, write a letter of the alphabet. This will serve as your key.

(2) On a separate piece of paper, write the name of the street you live on using numbers instead of words. For each letter of the word, use the number that is directly above it on your key.

(3) Exchange messages with a partner and use your key to decode your partner's information.

MATERIALS

- notebook
- small piece of paper

WHAT DO YOU THINK?

- How can information be coded?
- Under what types of circumstances would information need to be coded?

Electronics use coded information.

A code is a system of symbols used to send a message. Language is a code, for example. The symbols used in written language are lines and shapes. The words on this page represent meanings coded into the form of letters. As you read, your brain decodes the lines and shapes that make up each word, and you understand the message that is encoded.

An **electronic** device is a device that uses electric current to represent coded information. In electronics, the signals are variations in the current. Examples of electronic devices include computers, calculators, CD players, game systems, and more.

RESOURCE CENTER
CLASSZONE.COM

Find out more about electronics.

 CHECK YOUR READING Describe the signals used in electronic devices.

Binary Code

The English alphabet contains only 26 letters, yet there is no limit to the number of messages that can be expressed with it. That is because the message is conveyed not only by the letters that are chosen but also by the order in which they are placed.

Many electronic devices use a coding system with only two choices, as compared with the 26 in the alphabet. A coding system consisting of two choices is a **binary code.** As with a language, complex messages can be sent using binary code. In electronics, the two choices are whether an electric current is on or off. Switches in electronic circuits turn the current on and off. The result is a message represented in pulses of current.

It may be hard to imagine how something as complex as a computer game can be expressed with pulses of current. But it is a matter of breaking down information into smaller and smaller steps. You may have played the game 20 questions. In that game, you receive a message by asking someone only yes-or-no questions. The player answering the questions conveys the message only in *yes*'s and *no*'s, a binary code.

The diagram on the left shows how a decision-making process can be written in simple steps. The diagram is similar to a computer program, which tells a computer what to do. Each step of the process has been broken down into a binary question. If you determine exactly what you mean by *cold* and *hot,* then anyone using this program—or even a computer—would arrive at the same conclusion for a given set of conditions.

 How can a process be broken down into simple steps?

Digital Information

You can think of the yes-or-no choices in a binary system as being represented by the numbers 0 and 1. Information that is represented as numbers, or digits, is called **digital** information. In electronics, a circuit that is off is represented by 0, and a circuit that is on is represented by 1.

Digital information is represented in long streams of digits. Each 0 or 1 is also known as a bit, which is short for *binary digit.* A group of 8 bits is known as a byte. You might have heard the term *gigabyte* in reference to the amount of information that can be stored on a computer. One gigabyte is equal to about 1 billion bytes. That's 8 billion 0s and 1s!

Computers, digital cameras, CD players, DVD players, and other devices use digital information. Digital information is used in electronic devices more and more. There are at least two reasons for this:

- Digital information can be copied many times without losing its quality. The 1s are always copied as 1s, and the 0s are always copied as 0s.
- Digital information can be processed, or worked with, on computers.

For example, a photograph taken on a digital camera can be input to a computer in the form of digital information. Once the photograph is on a computer, the user can modify it, copy it, store it, and send it.

Many portable devices such as game systems and MP3 players can also be used with computers. Because computers and the devices use the same type of information, computers can be used to add games, music, and other programs to the devices. The photograph at right of a watch shows an example of a portable device that uses digital information.

This watch also functions as an MP3 player—it can store songs as digital files.

 Why is digital information often used in electronic devices?

INVESTIGATE Digital Information

How can you save a drawing in 1s and 0s?

PROCEDURE

1. Draw a 10-square by 10-square grid on a piece of graph paper.

2. Fill in some of the squares of the grid to draw a picture or pattern. Look at the example shown, but draw your own picture.

3. Starting in the upper left-hand corner of your grid, write 0 for every blank square and 1 for every filled-in square. Write a continuous series of 1s and 0s for all rows.

4. Exchange coded information with a partner who has not seen your picture. Draw a new grid in your notebook and fill it in using your partner's information.

WHAT DO YOU THINK?

- How were you able to reproduce your partner's picture?
- How is this activity similar to saving an image on a computer?

CHALLENGE Suppose you used three colored markers in your drawing—red, yellow, and green. How could you represent your color drawing using only 1s and 0s?

SKILL
Making models

MATERIALS
- graph paper
- plain paper

TIME
30 minutes

Analog to Digital

Some electronic devices use a system of coding electric current that differs from the digital code. Those electronics use analog information. **Analog** information is information that is represented in a continuous but varying form.

For example, a microphone records sound waves as analog information. The analog signal that is produced varies in strength as the sound wave varies in strength, as shown below. In order for the signal to be burned onto a CD, it is converted into digital information.

1 The sound waves are recorded in the microphone as an analog electrical signal.

2 The signal is sent through a computer circuit that measures, or samples, each part of the wave. The signal is sampled many thousands of times every second.

3 Each measurement of the wave is converted into a stream of digits. Microscopic pits representing the stream of digits are burned onto the CD. A stereo converts the signal from digital back to analog form, making it possible for people to hear what was recorded.

Analog and Digital Signals

Sound is recorded as an analog signal and converted to digital information for storage on a CD.

1 The sound wave is recorded as an analog signal.

analog signal

2 Each part of the analog signal is converted into a set of binary digits.

3 The stream of digits is burned onto the CD. The pits represent a stream of 1s, and the areas between the pits represent a stream of 0s.

digital signal

surface of CD

pit

CD burner

READING VISUALS What part of the illustration shows analog information? What part shows digital information?

Computer circuits process digital information.

A **computer** is an electronic device that processes digital information. Computers have been important in science and industry for a long time. Scientists use computers to gather, store, process, and share scientific data. As computers continue to get faster, smaller, and less expensive, they are turning up in many places.

Suppose you get a ride to the store. If the car you're riding in is a newer car, it probably has a computer inside it. At the store, you buy a battery, and the clerk records the sale on a register that is connected to a computer. You put the battery in your camera and take a picture, and the camera has a computer inside it.

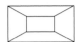
Integrated Circuits

The first digital computer weighed 30 tons and took up a whole room. After 60 years of development, computers the size of a postage stamp are able to complete the same tasks in less time. New technology in computer circuits has led to very small and powerful computers.

Computers process information on circuits that contain many switches, branches, and other elements that allow for a very fine control of current. An integrated circuit is a miniature electronic circuit. Tiny switches, called transistors, in these circuits turn off and on rapidly, signaling the stream of digits that represent information. Over a million of these switches may be on one small integrated circuit!

CHECK YOUR READING How do integrated circuits signal digital information?

Most integrated circuits are made from silicon, an element that is very abundant in Earth's crust. When silicon is treated with certain chemicals, it becomes a good semiconductor. A semiconductor is a material that is more conductive than an insulator but less conductive than a conductor. Silicon is a useful material in computers because the flow of current in it can be finely controlled.

Microscopic circuits are etched onto treated silicon with chemicals or lasers. Transistors and other circuit parts are constructed layer by layer on the silicon. A small, complex circuit on a single piece of silicon is known as a silicon chip, or microchip.

This integrated circuit is smaller than the common ant, *Camponotus pennsylvanicus*, which ranges in length from 6 to 17 mm.

Personal Computers

OUTLINE
Use an outline to take notes about personal computers.

I. Main idea
  A. Supporting idea
    1. Detail
    2. Detail
  B. Supporting idea

When you think of a computer, you probably think of a monitor, mouse, and keyboard—a personal computer (PC). All of the physical parts of a computer and its accessories are together known as hardware. Software refers to the instructions, or programs, and languages that control the hardware. The hardware, software, and user of a computer all work together to complete tasks.

CHECK YOUR READING What is the difference between hardware and software?

Computers have two kinds of memory. As the user is working, information is saved on the computer's random-access memory, or RAM. RAM is a computer's short-term memory. Most computers have enough RAM to store billions of bits. Another type of memory is called read-only memory, or ROM. ROM is a computer's long-term memory, containing the programs to start and run the computer. ROM can save information even after a computer is turned off.

The illustration below shows how a photograph is scanned, modified, and printed using a personal computer. The steps fall into four main functions—input, storage, processing, and output.

How a PC Works

Digital information can move through input, processing, storage, and output devices.

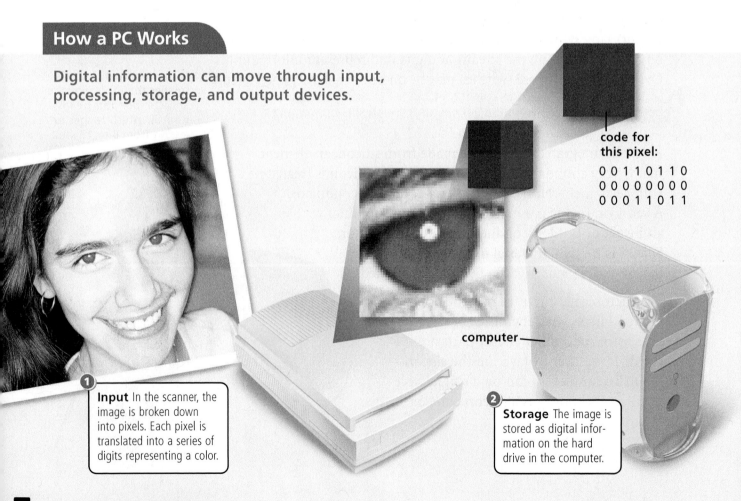

code for this pixel:
00110110
00000000
00011011

computer—

① **Input** In the scanner, the image is broken down into pixels. Each pixel is translated into a series of digits representing a color.

② **Storage** The image is stored as digital information on the hard drive in the computer.

① **Input** The user scans the photograph on a scanner. Each small area, or pixel, of the photograph is converted into a stream of digits. The digital information representing the photograph is sent to the main computer circuit, which is called the central processing unit, or CPU.

② **Storage** The user saves the photograph on a magnetic storage device called the hard drive. Small areas of the hard drive are magnetized in one of two directions. The magnetized areas oriented in one direction represent 1s, and the areas oriented in the opposite direction represent 0s, as a way to store the digital information.

③ **Processing** The photograph is converted back into pixels on the monitor, or screen, for the user to see. The computer below has a software program installed for altering photographs. The user adds more input to the computer with the mouse and the keyboard to improve the photograph.

④ **Output** The user sends the improved photograph to a printer. The printer converts the digital information back to pixels, and the photograph is printed.

VISUALIZATION
CLASSZONE.COM

See how hard drives store information.

CHECK YOUR READING During which one of the four main computer functions is information converted into digital information?

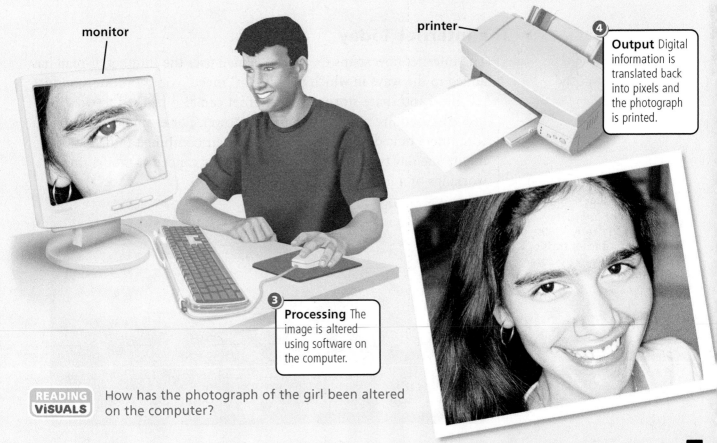

monitor

printer

④ **Output** Digital information is translated back into pixels and the photograph is printed.

③ **Processing** The image is altered using software on the computer.

READING VISUALS How has the photograph of the girl been altered on the computer?

Chapter 2: **Circuits and Electronics** 63 **E**

Computers can be linked with other computers.

You may have been at a computer lab or a library and had to wait for a printer to print something for you. Offices, libraries, and schools often have several computers that are all connected to the same printer. A group of computers that are linked together is known as a network. Computers can also be linked with other computers to share information. The largest network of computers is the Internet.

The Origin of the Internet

People have been using computer networks to share information on university campuses and military bases for decades. The computers within those networks were connected over telephone systems from one location to another. But those networks behaved like a series circuit. If the link to one computer was broken, the whole network of links went down.

The network that we now call the Internet is different. The United States Department of Defense formed the Internet by linking computers on college campuses across the country. Many extra links were formed, producing a huge web of connected computers. That way, if some links are broken, others still work.

 How does the Internet differ from earlier networks?

The Internet Today

The Internet now spans the world. E-mail uses the Internet. E-mail has added to the ways in which people can "meet," communicate, conduct business, and share stories. The Internet can also be used to work on tasks that require massive computing power. For example, millions of computers linked together, along with their combined information, might one day be used to develop a cure for cancer or model the workings of a human mind.

This map shows a representation of Internet traffic in the early 1990s. A map of Internet traffic now would be even more full of lines.

When you think of the Internet, you might think of the World Wide Web, or the Web. The Web consists of all of the information that can be accessed on the Internet. This information is stored on millions of host computers all over the world. The files that you locate are called Web pages. Each Web page has an address that begins with *www*, which stands for World Wide Web. The system allows you to search or surf through all of the information that is available on it. You might use the Web to research a project. Millions of people use the Web every day to find information, to shop, or for entertainment.

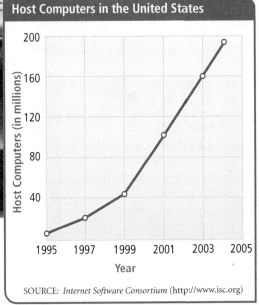

Host Computers in the United States

SOURCE: *Internet Software Consortium* (http://www.isc.org)

You may have heard of the Bronze Age or the Iron Age in your history class. Digital information and the Internet have had such a strong impact on the way we do things that some people refer to the era we live in as the Information Age.

2.3 Review

KEY CONCEPTS

1. Describe an example of coded information.

2. What is digital information? Give three examples of devices that use digital information.

3. Give an example of each of the following in terms of computers: input, storage, processing, and output.

CRITICAL THINKING

4. **Compare** Morse code uses a signal of dots and dashes to convey messages. How is Morse code similar to digital code?

5. **Infer** The word *integrated* means "brought together to form a whole." How does that definition apply to an integrated circuit?

○ CHALLENGE

6. **Predict** Computers as we know them did not exist 50 years ago, and now they are used for many purposes. How do you think people will use computers 50 years from now? Write a paragraph describing what you think the computers of the future will be like and how they will be used.

CHAPTER INVESTIGATION

Design an Electronic Communication Device

OVERVIEW AND PURPOSE
The telegraph was one of the first inventions to demonstrate that machines could be used to communicate over long distances. In a telegraph, messages are sent as electrical signals along a wire from a sending device to a receiver.

DESIGN — YOUR OWN —

Like modern computers, the telegraph uses a binary code. The code is called Morse code—a combination of short and long signals—to stand for letters and symbols. In this lab, you will use what you have learned about circuits to

- design a battery-powered device that uses Morse code
- build and test your design

▶ Problem

A toy company has contracted you to design and build a new product for kids. They want a communication device that is similar to a telegraph. Kids will use the device to communicate with each other in Morse code. The company's market research has shown that parents do not like noisy toys, so the company wants a device that uses light rather than sound as a signal.

MATERIALS
- 2 batteries
- light bulb in holder
- piece of copper wire
- 2 wire leads with alligator clips
- 2 craft sticks
- toothpick
- paper clip
- piece of cardboard
- clothespin
- aluminum foil
- rubber band
- scissors
- tape
- wire cutters
- Morse Code Chart

▶ Procedure

1. Brainstorm ideas for a communication device that can use Morse code. Look at the available materials and think how you could make a circuit that contains a light bulb and a switch.

2. Describe your proposed design and/or draw a sketch of it in your **Science Notebook.** Include a list of the materials that you would need to build it.

3 Show your design to a team member. Consider the constraints of each of your designs, such as what materials are available, the complexity of the design, and the time available.

4 Choose one idea or combine two ideas into a final design to test with your group. Build a sample version of your device, called a prototype.

5 Test your device by writing a short question. Translate the question into Morse code. Make long and short flashes of light on your device to send your message. Another person on your team should write down the message received in Morse code, translate the message, and send an answer.

6 Complete at least two trials. Each time, record the question in English, the question in code, the answer in code, and the answer in English.

7 Write a brief evaluation of how well the signal worked. Use the following criteria for your evaluation for each trial.

- What errors, if any, occurred while you were sending the signal?
- What errors, if any, occurred while you were receiving the signal?
- Did the translated answer make sense? Why or why not?

▶ Observe and Analyze   `Write It Up`

1. **MODEL** Draw a sketch of your final design. Label the parts. Next to your sketch, draw a circuit diagram of your device.

2. **INFER** How do the parts of your circuit allow you to control the flow of current?

3. **COMPARE** How is the signal that is used in your system similar to the digital information used by computers to process information? How does the signal differ?

4. **APPLY** A small sheet of instructions will be packaged with the device. Write a paragraph for the user that explains how to use it. Keep in mind that the user will probably be a child.

▶ Conclude   `Write It Up`

1. **EVALUATE** What problems, if any, did you encounter when testing your device? How might you improve upon the design?

2. **IDENTIFY LIMITS** What are the limitations of your design? You might consider its estimated costs, where and how kids will be able to use it, and the chances of the device breaking.

3. **APPLY** How might you modify your design so that it could be used by someone with limited vision?

4. **SYNTHESIZE** Write down the steps that you have used to develop this new product. Your first step was to brainstorm an idea.

▶ INVESTIGATE Further

CHALLENGE Design another system of communication that uses your own code. The signal should be in the form of flags. Make a table that lists what the signals mean and write instructions that explain how to use the system to communicate.

Design an Electronic Communication Device

Observe and Analyze

Table 1. Prototype Testing

	Trial 1	Trial 2
Question (English)		
Question (code)		
Answer (code)		
Answer (English)		
Evaluation		

Conclude

the BIG idea

Circuits control the flow of electric charge.

CONTENT REVIEW
CLASSZONE.COM

KEY CONCEPTS SUMMARY

2.1 Charge needs a continuous path to flow.

voltage source

switch

electrical device

conductor

Charge flows in a closed path. Circuits provide a closed path for current. Circuit parts include voltage sources, switches, conductors, and electrical devices such as resistors.

VOCABULARY
circuit p. 43
resistor p. 44
short circuit p. 46

2.2 Circuits make electric current useful.

Each device in a **series circuit** is wired on a single path.

Each device in a **parallel circuit** has its own connection to the voltage source.

VOCABULARY
series circuit p. 52
parallel circuit p. 53

2.3 Electronic technology is based on circuits.

Electronic devices use electrical signals to represent coded information. Computers process information in digital code which uses 1s and 0s to represent the information.

VOCABULARY
electronic p. 57
binary code p. 58
digital p. 58
analog p. 60
computer p. 61

Draw a Venn diagram for each of the term pairs below. Write the terms above the circles. In the center, write characteristics that the terms have in common. In the outer circles write the ways in which they differ. A sample diagram has been completed for you.

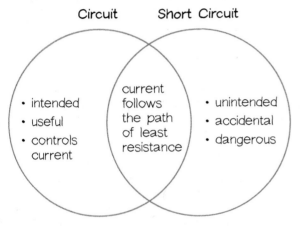

Circuit   Short Circuit

- intended
- useful
- controls current

current follows the path of least resistance

- unintended
- accidental
- dangerous

1. resistor; switch

2. series circuit; parallel circuit

3. digital; analog

4. digital; binary code

5. electronic; computer

Reviewing Key Concepts

Multiple Choice *Choose the letter of the best answer.*

6. Current always follows
   a. a path made of wire
   b. a path containing an electrical device
   c. a closed path
   d. an open circuit

7. When you open a switch in a circuit, you
   a. form a closed path for current
   b. reverse the current
   c. turn off its electrical devices
   d. turn on its electrical devices

8. Which one of the following parts of a circuit changes electrical energy into another form of energy?
   a. resistor
   b. conductor
   c. base
   d. voltage source

9. A circuit breaker is a safety device that
   a. must be replaced after each use
   b. has a wire that melts
   c. supplies voltage to a circuit
   d. stops the current

10. What happens when more than one voltage source is added to a circuit in series?
   a. The voltages are added together.
   b. The voltages cancel each other out.
   c. The voltages are multiplied together.
   d. The voltage of each source decreases.

11. Which of the following is an electronic device?
   a. flashlight
   b. calculator
   c. lamp
   d. electric fan

12. Which word describes the code used in digital technology?
   a. binary
   b. analog
   c. alphabetical
   d. Morse

13. Computers process information that has been
   a. broken down into simple steps
   b. converted into heat
   c. represented as a wave
   d. coded as an analog signal

Short Answer *Write a short answer to each question.*

14. How can hardware, software, and the user of a computer work together to complete a task?

15. Describe three parts of a personal computer and explain the main function of each.

Use the illustrations below to answer the next two questions.

16. PREDICT In which arrangement(s) above will the light bulb glow? For each arrangement in which you think the bulb will not glow, explain your reasoning.

17. APPLY Which arrangement could be used as a battery tester? List the materials that you would use to make a battery tester.

Use the diagram below to answer the next five questions.

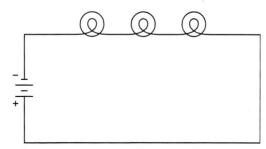

18. Is this a series circuit or a parallel circuit?

19. Explain what would happen if you unscrewed one of the bulbs in the circuit.

20. Explain what would happen if you wired three more bulbs into the circuit.

21. Draw and label a diagram of the same elements wired in the other type of circuit. Does your sketch involve more or fewer pieces of wire? How many?

22. Imagine you want to install a switch into your circuit. Where would you add the switch? Explain your answer.

23. ANALYZE Look for a pattern in the digital codes below, representing the numbers 1–10. What is the code for the number 11? How do you know?

0001; 0010; 0011; 0100; 0101;
0110; 0111; 1000; 1001; 1010

24. APPLY A computer circuit contains millions of switches that use temperature-dependent materials to operate lights, sounds, and a fan. How many different types of energy is current converted to in the computer circuit? Explain.

25. ANALYZE A music recording studio makes a copy of a CD that is itself a copy of another CD. Explain why the quality of the copied CDs is the same as the original CD.

26. INFER A new watch can be programmed to perform specific tasks. Describe what type of circuit the watch might contain.

27. SYNTHESIZE Explain how the Internet is like a worldwide parallel circuit.

the BIG idea

28. ANALYZE Look back at the photograph on pages 40–41. Think about the answer you gave to the question. How has your understanding of circuits changed?

29. SYNTHESIZE Explain how the following statement relates to electric circuits: "Energy can change from one form to another and can move from one place to another."

30. SUMMARIZE Write a paragraph summarizing how circuits control current. Using the heading at the top of page 43 as your topic sentence. Then give an example from each red and blue heading on pages 43–45.

UNIT PROJECTS

If you need to do an experiment for your unit project, gather the materials. Be sure to allow enough time to observe results before the project is due.

Interpreting Diagrams

The four circuit diagrams below use the standard symbols for the parts of a circuit.

A.   B.

C.

D.

Study the diagrams and answer the questions that follow.

1. Which diagram shows a series circuit, with one voltage source and two light bulbs?

  a. A   **c.** C

  b. B   **d.** D

2. Which diagram shows a parallel circuit powered by a battery, with three light bulbs?

  a. A   **c.** C

  b. B   **d.** D

3. The light bulbs in these diagrams limit the flow of charge and give off heat and light. Under which category of circuit parts do light bulbs belong?

  a. switches   **c.** resistors

  b. conductors   **d.** voltage sources

4. In which diagram would the light bulbs be dark?

  a. A   **c.** C

  b. B   **d.** D

5. If all light bulbs and voltage sources were equal, how would the light from each of the bulbs in diagram C compare to the light from each of the bulbs in diagram A?

  a. The bulbs in diagram C would give less light than the bulbs in diagram A.

  b. The bulbs in diagram C would give more light than the bulbs in diagram A.

  c. The bulbs in diagram C would give the same amount of light as the bulbs in diagram A.

  d. It cannot be determined which bulbs would give more light.

Extended Response

Answer the two questions below in detail. Include some of the terms from the word box. Underline each term you use in your answer.

flow of charge	electric current	binary code
open circuit	digital	signal

6. What are two types of safety devices designed to control electric current and prevent dangerous accidents? How does each work?

7. Explain how an electronic circuit differs from an electric circuit. What role do electronic circuits play in computer operations?

TIMELINES in Science

THE STORY OF ELECTRONICS

Inventions such as the battery, the dynamo, and the motor created a revolution in the production and use of electrical energy. Think of how many tools and appliances that people depend on every day run on electric current. Try to imagine not using electricity in any form for an entire day.

The use of electricity as an energy source only begins the story of how electricity has changed our lives. Parts of the story are shown on this timeline. Research in electronics has given us not only electrical versions of machines that already existed but also entirely new technologies.

These technologies include computers. Electricity is used as a signal inside computers to code and transmit information. Electricity can even mimic some of the processes of logical reasoning and decision making, giving computers the power to solve problems.

600 B.C.

Thales Studies Static Electricity

Greek philosopher-scientist Thales of Miletus discovers that when he rubs amber with wool or fur, the amber attracts feathers and straw. The Greek word for amber, *elektron*, is the origin of the word *electricity*.

EVENTS

| 640 B.C. | 620 B.C. | 600 B.C. | A.D. 1740 |

APPLICATIONS **AND** TECHNOLOGY

APPLICATION

Leyden Jar

In 1745 German inventor Ewald Georg von Kleist invented a device that would store a static charge. The device, called a Leyden jar, was a glass container filled with water. A wire ran from the outside of the jar through the cork into the water. The Leyden jar was the first capacitor, an electronic component that stores and releases charges. Capacitors have been key to the development of computers.

1752

Franklin Invents Lightning Rod

To test his hypothesis that lightning is caused by static electric charges, U.S. inventor Ben Franklin flies a kite during a thunderstorm. A metal key hangs from the kite strings. Sparks jump from the key to Franklin's knuckle, showing that the key has a static charge. On the basis of this experiment, Franklin invents the lightning rod.

1800

Volta Invents Battery

Italian scientist Alessandro Volta creates the first battery by stacking round plates of metal separated by disks soaked in salt water. Volta's discovery refutes the competing belief that electricity must be created by living beings.

1776

Bassi Gives Physics a Boost

Italian scholar Laura Bassi, one of the first women to hold a chair at a major European university, is named professor of experimental physics. Bassi uses her position to establish one of the world's first electrical laboratories.

1760   1780   1800   1820   1840

TECHNOLOGY

The Difference Engine

Around 1822 British mathematician Charles Babbage developed the first prototype of a machine that could perform calculations mechanically. Babbage's "difference engine" used disks connected to rods with hand cranks to calculate mathematical tables. Babbage's invention came more than 100 years before the modern computer.

1879
Edison Improves Dynamo

To help bring electric lights to the streets of New York City, U.S. inventor Thomas Edison develops an improved dynamo, or generator. Edison's dynamo, known as a long-legged Mary Ann, operates at about twice the efficiency of previous models.

1904
Vacuum Tube Makes Debut

British inventor Ambrose Fleming modifies a light bulb to create an electronic vacuum tube. Fleming's tube, which he calls a valve, allows current to flow in one direction but not the other and can be used to detect weak radio signals.

1947
Transistor Invented

A transistor—a tiny electronic switch made out of a solid material called a semiconductor—is introduced to regulate the flow of electricity. Transistors, which do not produce excess heat and never burn out, can replace the vacuum tube in electronic circuitry and can be used to make smaller, cheaper, and more powerful computers.

| 1860 | 1880 | 1900 | 1920 | 1940 |

APPLICATION

First Electronic Digital Computer

Electronic Numerical Integrator and Computer (ENIAC) was the first digital computer. It was completed and installed in 1944 at the Moore School of Electrical Engineering at the University of Pennsylvania. Weighing more than 30 tons, ENIAC contained 19,000 vacuum tubes, 70,000 resistors, and 6000 switches, and it used almost 200 kilowatts of electric power. ENIAC could perform 5000 additions per second.

1958

Chip Inventors Think Small

Jack Kilby, a U.S. electrical engineer, conceives the idea of making an entire circuit out of a single piece of germanium. The integrated circuit, or "computer chip," is born. This invention enables computers and other electronic devices to be made much smaller than before.

2001

Scientists Shrink Circuits to Atomic Level

Researchers succeed in building a logic circuit, a kind of transistor the size of a single molecule. The molecule, a tube of carbon atoms called a carbon nanotube, can be as small as 10 atoms across—500 times smaller than previous transistors. Computer chips, which currently contain over 40 million transistors, could hold hundreds of millions or even billions of nanotube transistors.

RESOURCE CENTER
CLASSZONE.COM

Explore current research in electronics and computers.

1960   1980   2000

TECHNOLOGY

Miniaturization

Miniaturization has led to an explosion of computer technology. As circuits have shrunk, allowing more components in less space, computers have become smaller and more powerful. They have also become easier to integrate with other technologies, such as telecommunications. When not being used for a phone call, this cell phone can be used to connect to the Internet, to access e-mail, and even to play computer games.

SPOTLIGHT on
LEWIS LATIMER

Lewis Latimer (1848–1928) made many improvements to electrical technology. At an early age, he taught himself mechanical drafting. In 1876 he helped Alexander Graham Bell with the drawings for the first telephone. Bell needed the drawings to file for a patent. Latimer is best known for his work with the light bulb. He improved how carbon filaments were made. His filaments lasted longer than the ones made by Thomas Edison.

Latimer later went to work for Edison's lighting company. He became an expert on electric lighting systems and many sought his advice. He always tried to help others. In addition to his professional work, Latimer taught mechanical drawing to immigrants.

ACTIVITIES

Reliving History

Make a Leyden jar capacitor. Line the inside of a jar with aluminum foil. Stop the jar with clay. Insert a copper wire through the plug so that one end touches the foil and the other sticks out of the jar about 2 centimeters.

To test for a voltage difference between the wire and the glass, touch one end of a multimeter to the exposed wire and the other end to the glass. Run a comb through your hair several times and touch it to the wire. Test the voltage difference again.

Writing About Science

Learn more about the current state of electronic circuit miniaturization. Write up the results of your research in the form of a magazine article.

CHAPTER

Magnetism

the **BIG** idea

Current can produce magnetism, and magnetism can produce current.

Key Concepts

SECTION

3.1 Magnetism is a force that acts at a distance.
Learn how magnets exert forces.

SECTION

3.2 Current can produce magnetism.
Learn about electromagnets and their uses.

SECTION

3.3 Magnetism can produce current.
Learn how magnetism can produce an electric current.

SECTION

3.4 Generators supply electrical energy.
Learn how generators are used in the production of electrical energy.

Internet Preview

CLASSZONE.COM

Chapter 3 online resources: Content Review, Simulation, Visualization, three Resource Centers, Math Tutorial, Test Practice

EXPLORE (the BIG idea)

Is It Magnetic?

Experiment with a magnet and several objects made of different materials.

Observe and Think
Which objects are attracted to the magnet? Why do you think the magnet attracts some objects and not others?

What force is acting on this compass needle?

How Can You Make a Chain?

Hang a paper clip on the end of a magnet. Then hang a second paper clip by touching it to the end of the first paper clip. Add more paper clips to make a chain.

Observe and Think How many paper clips did you add? What held the chain together?

Internet Activity: Electromagnets

Go to **ClassZone.com** to work with a virtual electromagnet. Explore how current and magnetism are related.

Observe and Think
What happens when you increase the voltage?

NSTA
scilinks.org
SCiLINKS

Electromagnetism **Code: MDL067**

Getting Ready to Learn

◀ CONCEPT REVIEW

- Energy can change from one form to another.
- A force is a push or a pull.
- Power is the rate of energy transfer.

◀ VOCABULARY REVIEW

electric current p. 28

circuit p. 43

kinetic energy *See Glossary.*

 CONTENT REVIEW
CLASSZONE.COM
Review concepts and vocabulary.

▶ TAKING NOTES

MAIN IDEA WEB

Write each new blue heading in a box. Then write notes in boxes around the center box that give important terms and details about that blue heading.

VOCABULARY STRATEGY

Place each vocabulary term at the center of a **description wheel** diagram. As you read about the term, write some words describing it on the spokes.

See the Note-Taking Handbook on pages R45–R51.

SCIENCE NOTEBOOK

Magnetism is the force exerted by magnets.

All magnets have two poles.

Magnets attract and repel other magnets.

Opposite poles attract, and like poles repel.

Magnets have magnetic fields of force around them.

Magnetic fields of atoms point in the same direction.

In magnets, they line up.

MAGNETIC DOMAINS

Nonmagnetic materials don't have them.

Magnetic materials have them.

Magnetism is a force that acts at a distance.

◀ **BEFORE, you learned**

- A force is a push or pull
- Some forces act at a distance
- Atoms contain charged particles

▶ **NOW, you will learn**

- How magnets attract and repel other magnets
- What makes some materials magnetic
- Why a magnetic field surrounds Earth

VOCABULARY

magnet p. 79
magnetism p. 80
magnetic pole p. 80
magnetic field p. 81
magnetic domain p. 82

EXPLORE Magnetism

How do magnets behave?

PROCEDURE

1. Clamp the clothespin on the dowel so that it makes a stand for the magnets, as shown.

2. Place the three magnets on the dowel. If there is a space between pairs of magnets, measure and record the distance between them.

3. Remove the top magnet, turn it over, and replace it on the dowel. Record your observations. Experiment with different arrangements of the magnets and record your observations.

MATERIALS

- clothespin
- wooden dowel
- 3 disk magnets
- ruler

WHAT DO YOU THINK?

- How did the arrangement of the magnets affect their behavior?
- What evidence indicates that magnets exert a force?

Magnets attract and repel other magnets.

Suppose you get home from school and open the refrigerator to get some milk. As you close the door, it swings freely until it suddenly seems to close by itself. There is a magnet inside the refrigerator door that pulls it shut. A **magnet** is an object that attracts certain other materials, particularly iron and steel.

There may be quite a few magnets in your kitchen. Some are obvious, like the seal of the refrigerator and the magnets that hold notes to its door. Other magnets run the motor in a blender, provide energy in a microwave oven, operate the speakers in a radio on the counter, and make a doorbell ring.

VOCABULARY
Make a description wheel for the term *magnet*.

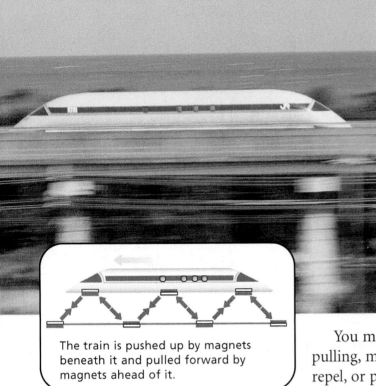

Magnetism

The force exerted by a magnet is called **magnetism.** The push or pull of magnetism can act at a distance, which means that the magnet does not have to touch an object to exert a force on it. When you close the refrigerator, you feel the pull before the magnet actually touches the metal frame. There are other forces that act at a distance, including gravity and static electricity. Later you will read how the force of magnetism is related to electricity. In fact, magnetism is the result of a moving electric charge.

The train is pushed up by magnets beneath it and pulled forward by magnets ahead of it.

You may be familiar with magnets attracting, or pulling, metal objects toward them. Magnets can also repel, or push away, objects. The train in the photograph at the left is called a maglev train. The word *maglev* is short for *maglev levitation*, or lifting up. As you can see in the diagram, the train does not touch the track. Magnetism pushes the entire train up and pulls it forward. Maglev trains can move as fast as 480 kilometers per hour (300 mi/h).

 CHECK YOUR READING How can a train operate without touching the track?

Magnetic Poles

RESOURCE CENTER
CLASSZONE.COM

Find out more about magnetism.

The force of magnetism is not evenly distributed throughout a magnet. **Magnetic poles** are the parts of a magnet where the magnetism is the strongest. Every magnet has two magnetic poles. If a bar magnet is suspended so that it can swing freely, one pole of the magnet always points toward the north. That end of the magnet is known as the north-seeking pole, or north pole. The other end of the magnet is called the south pole. Many magnets are marked with an *N* and an *S* to indicate the poles.

As with electric charges, opposite poles of a magnet attract and like poles—or poles that are the same—repel, or push each other away. Every magnet has both a north pole and a south pole. A horseshoe magnet is like a bar magnet that has been bent into the shape of a *U*. It has a pole at each of its ends. If you

break a bar magnet between the two poles, the result is two smaller magnets, each of which has a north pole and a south pole. No matter how many times you break a magnet, the result is smaller magnets.

Magnetic Fields

You have read that magnetism is a force that can act at a distance. However magnets cannot exert a force on an object that is too far away. A **magnetic field** is the region around a magnet in which the magnet exerts force. If a piece of iron is within the magnetic field of a magnet, it will be pulled toward the magnet. Many small pieces of iron, called iron filings, are used to show the magnetic field around a magnet. The iron filings form a pattern of lines called magnetic field lines.

READING TiP

Thin red lines in the illustrations below indicate the magnetic field.

The Magnetic Field Around a Magnet

The arrangement of the magnetic field lines depends on the shape of the magnet, but the lines always extend from one pole to the other pole. The magnetic field lines are always shown as starting from the north pole and ending at the south pole. In the illustrations above, you can see that the lines are closest together near the magnets' poles. That is where the force is strongest. The force is weaker farther away from the magnet.

 CHECK YOUR READING Where is the magnetic field of a magnet the strongest?

What happens to the magnetic fields of two magnets when the magnets are brought together? As you can see below, each magnet has an effect on the field of the other magnet. If the magnets are held so that the north pole of one magnet is close to the south pole of the other, the magnetic field lines extend from one magnet to the other. The magnets pull together. On the other hand, if both north poles or both south poles of two magnets are brought near one another, the magnets repel. It is very difficult to push like poles of strong magnets together because magnetic repulsion pushes them apart.

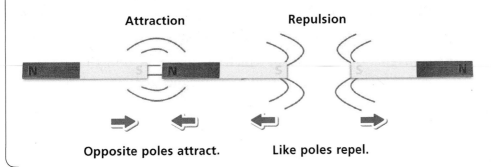

Opposite poles attract.   Like poles repel.

Some materials are magnetic.

Some magnets occur naturally. Lodestone is a type of mineral that is a natural magnet and formed the earliest magnets that people used. The term *magnet* comes from the name *Magnesia,* a region of Greece where lodestone was discovered. Magnets can also be made from materials that contain certain metallic elements, such as iron.

If you have ever tried picking up different types of objects with a magnet, you have seen that some materials are affected by the magnet and other materials are not. Iron, nickel, cobalt, and a few other metals have properties that make them magnetic. Other materials, such as wood, cannot be made into magnets and are not affected by magnets. Whether a material is magnetic or not depends on its atoms—the particles that make up all matter.

You read in Chapter 1 that the protons and electrons of an atom have electric fields. Every atom also has a weak magnetic field, produced by the electron's motion around a nucleus. In addition, each electron spins around its axis, an imaginary line through its center. The spinning motion of the electrons in magnetic materials increases the strength of the magnetic field around each atom. The magnetic effect of one electron is usually cancelled by another electron that spins in the opposite direction.

Inside Magnetic Materials

READING TIP

The red arrows in the illustration on page 83 are tiny magnetic fields.

The illustration on page 83 shows how magnets and the materials they affect differ from other materials.

1. In a material that is not magnetic, such as wood, the magnetic fields of the atoms are weak and point in different directions. The magnetic fields cancel each other out. As a result, the overall material is not magnetic and could not be made into a magnet.

2. In a material that is magnetic, such as iron, the magnetic fields of a group of atoms align, or point in the same direction. A **magnetic domain** is a group of atoms whose magnetic fields are aligned. The domains of a magnetic material are not themselves aligned, so their fields cancel one another out. Magnetic materials are pulled by magnets and can be made into magnets.

3. A magnet is a material in which the magnetic domains are all aligned. The material is said to be magnetized.

CHECK YOUR READING How do magnets differ from materials that are not magnetic?

How Magnets Differ from Other Materials

Magnets, and the materials they attract, contain small regions called magnetic domains. In a magnet, the domains are aligned.

Nonmagnetic Materials

Magnet

Magnetic Materials

① Nonmagnetic Materials

Some materials, like wood, are not magnetic. The tiny magnetic fields of their spinning electrons point in different directions and cancel each other out.

② Magnetic Materials

magnetic domain

Other materials, like iron, are magnetic. Magnetic materials have magnetic domains, but the fields of the domains point in different directions.

③ Magnets

When a material is magnetized, the magnetic fields of all the domains point in the same direction.

READING VISUALS Do the paper clips in this photograph contain magnetic domains? Why or why not?

Temporary and Permanent Magnets

If you bring a magnet near a paper clip that contains iron, the paper clip is pulled toward the magnet. As the magnet nears the paper clip, the domains within the paper clip are attracted to the magnet's nearest pole. As a result, the domains within the paper clip become aligned. The paper clip develops its own magnetic field.

You can make a chain of paper clips that connect to one another through these magnetic fields. However, if you remove the magnet, the chain falls apart. The paper clips are temporary magnets, and their domains return to a random arrangement when the stronger magnetic field is removed.

Placing magnetic materials in very strong magnetic fields makes permanent magnets, such as the ones you use in the experiments in this chapter. You can make a permanent magnet by repeatedly stroking a piece of magnetic material in the same direction with a strong magnet. This action aligns the domains. However, if you drop a permanent magnet, or expose it to high temperatures, some of the domains can be shaken out of alignment, weakening its magnetism.

 CHECK YOUR READING How can you make a permanent magnet?

Earth is a magnet.

People discovered long ago that when a piece of lodestone was allowed to turn freely, one end always pointed toward the north. Hundreds of years ago, sailors used lodestone in the first compasses for navigation. A compass works because Earth itself is a large magnet. A compass is simply a magnet that is suspended so that it can turn freely. The magnetic field of the compass needle aligns itself with the much larger magnetic field of Earth.

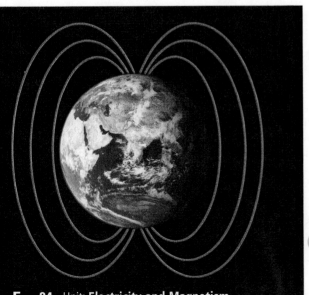

Earth's Magnetic Field

The magnetic field around Earth acts as if there were a large bar magnet that runs through Earth's axis. Earth's axis is the imaginary line through the center of Earth around which it rotates. The source of the magnetic field that surrounds Earth is the motion of its core, which is composed mostly of iron and nickel. Charged particles flow within the core. Scientists have proposed several explanations of how that motion produces the magnetic field, but the process is not yet completely understood.

 CHECK YOUR READING What is the source of Earth's magnetic field?

INVESTIGATE Earth's Magnetic Field

What moves a compass needle?

PROCEDURE

1. Gently place the aluminum foil on the water so that it floats.

2. Rub one pole of the magnet along the needle, from one end of the needle to the other. Lift up the magnet and repeat. Do this about 25 times, rubbing in the same direction each time. Place the magnet far away from your set-up.

3. Gently place the needle on the floating foil to act as a compass.

4. Turn the foil so that the needle points in a different direction. Observe what happens when you release the foil.

WHAT DO YOU THINK?

- What direction did the needle move when you placed it in the bowl?

- What moved the compass's needle?

CHALLENGE How could you use your compass to answer a question of your own about magnetism?

SKILL FOCUS
Inferring

MATERIALS
- small square of aluminum foil
- bowl of water
- strong magnet
- sewing needle

TIME

15 minutes

Earth's magnetic field affects all the magnetic materials around you. Even the cans of food in your cupboard are slightly magnetized by this field. Hold a compass close to the bottom of a can and observe what happens. The magnetic domains in the metal can have aligned and produced a weak magnetic field. If you twist the can and check it again several days later, you can observe the effect of the domains changing their alignment.

Sailors learned many centuries ago that the compass does not point exactly toward the North Pole of Earth's axis. Rather, the compass magnet is currently attracted to an area 966 kilometers (600 mi) from the end of the axis of rotation. This area is known as the magnetic north pole. Interestingly, the magnetic poles of Earth can reverse, so that the magnetic north pole becomes the magnetic south pole. This has happened at least 400 times over the last 330 million years. The most recent reversal was about 780,000 years ago.

The evidence that the magnetic north and south poles reverse is found in rocks in which the minerals contain iron. The iron in the minerals lines up with Earth's magnetic field as the rock forms. Once the rock is formed, the domains remain in place. The evidence for the reversing magnetic field is shown in layers of rocks on the ocean floor, where the domains are arranged in opposite directions.

Magnetism and the Atmosphere

A constant stream of charged particles is released by reactions inside the Sun. These particles could be damaging to living cells if they reached the surface of Earth. One important effect of Earth's magnetic field is that it turns aside, or deflects, the flow of the charged particles.

Observers view a beautiful display of Northern Lights in Alaska.

Many of the particles are deflected toward the magnetic poles, where Earth's magnetic field lines are closest together. As the particles approach Earth, they react with oxygen and nitrogen in Earth's atmosphere. These interactions can be seen at night as vast, moving sheets of color—red, blue, green or violet—that can fill the whole sky. These displays are known as the Northern Lights or the Southern Lights.

 CHECK YOUR READING Why do the Northern Lights and the Southern Lights occur near Earth's magnetic poles?

3.1 Review

KEY CONCEPTS

1. What force causes magnets to attract or repel one another?

2. Why are some materials magnetic and not others?

3. Describe three similarities between Earth and a bar magnet.

CRITICAL THINKING

4. **Apply** A needle is picked up by a magnet. What can you say about the needle's atoms?

5. **Infer** The Northern Lights can form into lines in the sky. What do you think causes this effect?

CHALLENGE

6. **Infer** Hundreds of years ago sailors observed that as they traveled farther north, their compass needle tended to point toward the ground as well as toward the north. What can you conclude about the magnet inside Earth from this observation?

Think SCIENCE

Can Magnets Heal People?

Many people believe that a magnetic field can relieve pain and cure injuries or illnesses. They point out that human blood cells contain iron and that magnets attract iron.

▶ Claims

Here are some claims from advertisements and published scientific experiments.

a. In an advertisement, a person reported back pain that went away overnight when a magnetic pad was taped to his back.

b. In an advertisement, a person used magnets to treat a painful bruise. The pain reportedly stopped soon after the magnet was applied.

c. In a research project, people who had recovered from polio, but still had severe pain, rated the amount of pain they experienced. People who used magnets reported slightly more pain relief than those who used fake magnets that looked like the real magnets.

d. A research project studied people with severe muscle pain. Patients who slept on magnetic pads for six months reported slightly less pain than those who slept on nonmagnetic pads or no pads.

e. A research project studied people with pain in their heels, placing magnets in their shoes. About sixty percent of people with real magnets reported improvements. About sixty percent of people with fake magnets also reported improvements.

▶ Controls

Scientists use control groups to determine whether a change was a result of the experimental variable or some other cause. A control group is the same as an experimental group in every way except for the variable that is tested. For each of the above cases, was a control used? If not, can you think of some other explanation for the result?

▶ Evaluating Conclusions

On Your Own Evaluate each claim or report separately. Based on all the evidence, can you conclude that magnets are useful for relieving pain? What further evidence would help you decide?

As a Group Find advertisements for companies that sell magnets for medical use. Do they provide information about how their tests were conducted and how you can contact the doctors or scientists involved?

CHALLENGE Design an experiment, with controls, that would show whether or not magnets are useful for relieving pain.

Some people believe that pads containing magnets, such as these, can relieve pain.

Current can produce magnetism.

BEFORE, you learned	NOW, you will learn
• Electric current is the flow of charge • Magnetism is a force exerted by magnets • Magnets attract or repel other magnets	• How an electric current can produce a magnetic field • How electromagnets are used • How motors use electro-magnets

VOCABULARY

electromagnetism p. 89
electromagnet p. 90

EXPLORE Magnetism from Electric Current

What is the source of magnetism?

PROCEDURE

1. Tape one end of the wire to the battery.

2. Place the compass on the table. Place the wire so that it is lying beside the compass, parallel to the needle of the compass. Record your observations.

3. Briefly touch the free end of the wire to the other end of the battery. Record your observations.

4. Turn the battery around and tape the other end to the wire. Repeat steps 2 and 3.

WHAT DO YOU THINK?
• What did you observe?
• What is the relationship between the direction of the battery and the direction of the compass needle?

MATERIALS
• electrical tape
• copper wire
• AA cell (battery)
• compass

An electric current produces a magnetic field.

REMINDER

Current is the flow of electrons through a conductor.

Like many discoveries, the discovery that electric current is related to magnetism was unexpected. In the 1800s, a Danish physicist named Hans Christian Oersted (UR-stehd) was teaching a physics class. Oersted used a battery and wire to demonstrate some properties of electricity. He noticed that as an electric charge passed through the wire, the needle of a nearby compass moved.

When he turned the current off, the needle returned to its original direction. After more experiments, Oersted confirmed that there is a relationship between magnetism and electricity. He discovered that an electric current produces a magnetic field.

Electromagnetism

The relationship between electric current and magnetism plays an important role in many modern technologies. **Electromagnetism** is magnetism that results from an electric current. When a charged particle such as an electron moves, it produces a magnetic field. Because an electric current generally consists of moving electrons, a current in a wire produces a magnetic field. In fact, the wire acts as a magnet. Increasing the amount of current in the wire increases the strength of the magnetic field.

VOCABULARY
Remember to record *electromagnetism* in your notebook.

You have seen how magnetic field lines can be drawn around a magnet. The magnetic field lines around a wire are usually illustrated as a series of circles. The magnetic field of a wire actually forms the shape of a tube around the wire. The direction of the current determines the direction of the magnetic field. If the direction of the electric current is reversed, the magnetic field still exists in circles around the wire, but is reversed.

magnetic field

current-carrying wire

If the wire is shaped into a loop, the magnetism becomes concentrated inside the loop. The field is much stronger in the middle of the loop than it is around a straight wire. If you wind the wire into a coil, the magnetic force becomes stronger with each additional turn of wire as the magnetic field becomes more concentrated.

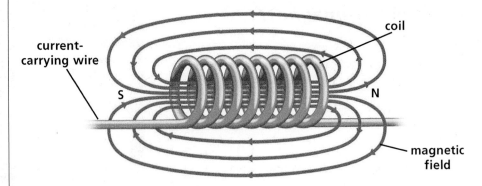

current-carrying wire

coil

S   N

magnetic field

A coil of wire with charge flowing through it has a magnetic field that is similar to the magnetic field of a bar magnet. Inside the coil, the field flows in one direction, forming a north pole at one end. The flow outside the coil returns to the south pole. The direction of the electric current in the wire determines which end of the coil becomes the north pole.

 CHECK YOUR READING How is a coil of wire that carries a current similar to a bar magnet?

Making an Electromagnet

Recall that a piece of iron in a strong magnetic field becomes a magnet itself. An **electromagnet** is a magnet made by placing a piece of iron or steel inside a coil of wire. As long as the coil carries a current, the metal acts as a magnet and increases the magnetic field of the coil. But when the current is turned off, the magnetic domains in the metal become random again and the magnetic field disappears.

By increasing the number of loops in the coil, you can increase the strength of the electromagnet. Electromagnets exert a much more powerful magnetic field than a coil of wire without a metal core. They can also be much stronger than the strongest permanent magnets made of metal alone. You can increase the field strength of an electromagnet by adding more coils or a stronger current. Some of the most powerful magnets in the world are huge electromagnets that are used in scientific instruments.

 CHECK YOUR READING   How can you increase the strength of an electromagnet?

INVESTIGATE Electromagnets

How can you make an electromagnet?

PROCEDURE

1. Starting about 25 cm from one end of the wire, wrap the wire in tight coils around the nail. The coils should cover the nail from the head almost to the point.

2. Tape the two batteries together as shown. Tape one end of the wire to a free battery terminal.

3. Touch the point of the nail to a paper clip and record your observations.

4. Connect the other end of the wire to the other battery terminal. Again touch the point of the nail to a paper clip. Disconnect the wire from the battery. Record your observations.

WHAT DO YOU THINK?

- What did you observe?
- Did you make an electromagnet? How do you know?

CHALLENGE Do you think the result would be different if you used an aluminum nail instead of an iron nail? Why?

SKILL FOCUS
Observing

MATERIALS
- insulated wire
- large iron nail
- 2 D cells
- electrical tape
- paper clip

TIME
20 minutes

Uses of Electromagnets

Because electromagnets can be turned on and off, they have more uses than permanent magnets. The photograph below shows a powerful electromagnet on a crane. While the electric charge flows through the coils of the magnet, it lifts hundreds of cans at a recycling plant. When the crane operator turns off the current, the magnetic field disappears and the cans drop from the crane.

A permanent magnet would not be nearly as useful for this purpose. Although you could use a large permanent magnet to lift the cans, it would be hard to remove them from the magnet.

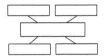
MAIN IDEA WEB
Make a main idea web for the uses of electromagnets.

This powerful electromagnet can be turned on and off to collect and move cans at a recycling plant.

wire supplying electric current

electromagnet

You use an electromagnet every time you store information on a computer. The computer hard drive contains disks that have billions of tiny magnetic domains in them. When you save a file, a tiny electromagnet in the computer is activated. The magnetic field of the electromagnet changes the orientation of the small magnetic domains. The small magnets store your file in a form that can be read later by the computer. A similar system is used to store information on magnetic tape of an audiocassette or videocassette. Sound and pictures are stored on the tape by the arrangement of magnets embedded in the plastic film.

Magnetic information is often stored on credit cards and cash cards. A black strip on the back of the card contains information about the account number and passwords. The cards can be damaged if they are frequently exposed to magnetic fields. For example, cards should not be stored with their strips facing each other, or near a magnetic clasp on a purse or wallet. These magnetic fields can change the arrangement of the tiny magnetic domains on the card and erase the stored information.

Operation

Motors use electromagnets.

Because magnetism is a force, magnets can be used to move things. Electric motors convert the energy of an electric current into motion by taking advantage of the interaction between current and magnetism.

There are hundreds of devices that contain electric motors. Examples include power tools, electrical kitchen appliances, and the small fans in a computer. Almost anything with moving parts that uses current has an electric motor.

Motors

See a motor in motion.

Page 93 shows how a simple motor works. The photograph at the top of the page shows a motor that turns the blades of a fan. The illustration in the middle of the page shows the main parts of a simple motor. Although they may look different from each other, all motors have similar parts and work in a similar way. The main parts of an electrical motor include a voltage source, a shaft, an electromagnet, and at least one additional magnet. The shaft of the motor turns other parts of the device.

Recall that an electromagnet consists of a coil of wire with current flowing through it. Find the electromagnet in the illustration on page 93. The electromagnet is placed between the poles of another magnet.

When current from the voltage source flows through the coil, a magnetic field is produced around the electromagnet. The poles of the magnet interact with the poles of the electromagnet, causing the motor to turn.

1 The poles of the magnet push on the like poles of the electromagnet, causing the electromagnet to turn.

2 As the motor turns, the opposite poles pull on each other.

3 When the poles of the electromagnet line up with the opposite poles of the magnet, a part of the motor called the commutator reverses the polarity of the electromagnet. Now, the poles push on each other again and the motor continues to turn.

The illustration of the motor on page 93 is simplified so that you can see all of the parts. If you saw the inside of an actual motor, it might look like the illustration on the left. Notice that the wire is coiled many times. The electromagnet in a strong motor may coil hundreds of times. The more coils, the stronger the motor.

coil of wire   magnet

shaft

CHECK YOUR READING What causes the electromagnet in a motor to turn?

How a Motor Works

Although motors may look different from each other, they all have similar parts and work in a similar way.

motor in fan

electromagnet   shaft

voltage source

commutator

shaft

magnet

electromagnet

The commutator rotates along with the electromagnet, causing the electromagnet's poles to switch with every half-rotation.

① Like poles of the magnets push on each other.

② As the motor turns, opposite poles attract.

③ The electromagnet's poles are switched, and like poles again repel.

 READING VISUALS Would a motor work without an electromagnet? Why or why not?

Uses of Motors

Many machines and devices contain electric motors that may not be as obvious as the motor that turns the blades of a fan, for example. Even though the motion produced by the motor is circular, motors can move objects in any direction. For example, electric motors move power windows in a car up and down.

Motor B moves a laser across the CD.

These gears change the rotational motion of the motor into a straight motion.

laser

Motor A turns the CD.

Motors can be very large, such as the motors that power an object as large as a subway train. They draw electric current from a third rail on the track or wires overhead that carry electric current. A car uses an electric current to start the engine. When the key is turned, a circuit is closed, producing a current from the battery to the motor. Other motors are very small, like the battery-operated motors that move the hands of a wristwatch.

The illustration on the left shows the two small motors in a portable CD player. Motor A causes the CD to spin. Motor B is connected to a set of gears. The gears convert the rotational motion of the motor into a straight-line motion, or linear motion. As the CD spins, a laser moves straight across the CD from the center outward. The laser reads the information on the CD. The motion from Motor B moves the laser across the CD.

CHECK YOUR READING Explain the function served by each motor in a CD player.

3.2 Review

KEY CONCEPTS

1. Explain how electric current and magnetism are related.

2. Describe three uses of electromagnets.

3. Explain how electrical energy is converted to motion in a motor.

CRITICAL THINKING

4. **Contrast** How does an electromagnet differ from a permanent magnet?

5. **Apply** Provide examples of two things in your home that use electric motors, and explain why they are easier to use because of the motors.

⬤ CHALLENGE

6. **Infer** Why is it necessary to change the direction of the current in the coil of an electric motor as it turns?

3.3 Magnetism can produce current.

◀ **BEFORE,** you learned

- Magnetism is a force exerted by magnets
- Electric current can produce a magnetic field
- Electromagnets can make objects move

▶ **NOW,** you will learn

- How a magnetic field can produce an electric current
- How a generator converts energy
- How direct current and alternating current differ

VOCABULARY

generator p. 96
direct current p. 97
alternating current p. 97
transformer p. 99

EXPLORE Energy Conversion

How can a motor produce current?

PROCEDURE

1. Touch the wires on the motor to the battery terminals to see how the motor operates.

2. Connect the wires to the light bulb.

3. Roll the shaft, or the movable part of the motor, between your fingers. Observe the light bulb.

4. Now spin the shaft rapidly. Record your observations.

WHAT DO YOU THINK?
- How did you produce current?
- What effect did your motion have on the amount of light produced?

MATERIALS
- small motor
- AA cell (battery)
- light bulb in holder

Magnets are used to generate an electric current.

MAIN IDEA WEB
Make a main idea web in your notebook for this heading.

In the 1830s, about ten years after Oersted discovered that an electric current produces magnetism, physicists observed the reverse effect—a moving magnetic field induces an electric current. When a magnet moves inside a coiled wire that is in a circuit, an electric current is generated in the wire.

It is often easier to generate an electric current by moving a wire inside a magnetic field. Whether it is the magnet or the wire that moves, the effect is the same. Current is generated as long as the wire crosses the magnetic field lines.

 CHECK YOUR READING What must happen for a magnetic field to produce an electric current?

Generating an Electric Current

A **generator** is a device that converts the energy of motion, or kinetic energy, into electrical energy. A generator is similar to a motor in reverse. If you manually turn the shaft of a motor that contains a magnet, you can produce electric current.

The illustration below shows a portable generator that provides electrical energy to charge a cell phone in an emergency. The generator produces current as you turn the handle. Because it does not need to be plugged in, the generator can be used wherever and whenever it is needed to recharge a phone. The energy is supplied by the person turning the handle.

❶ As the handle is turned, it rotates a series of gears. The gears turn the shaft of the generator.

❷ The rotation of the shaft causes coils of wire to rotate within a magnetic field.

❸ As the coils of the wire cross the magnetic field line, electric current is generated. The current recharges the battery of the cell phone.

CHECK YOUR READING What is the source of energy for a cell phone generator?

How a Cell Phone Generator Works

An emergency cell phone charger uses a generator to produce electric current.

❸ Electric current recharges the phone's battery.

❶ Turning the handle provides kinetic energy to the generator, making the gears rotate.

❷ The turning motion rotates coils of wire inside a magnet. This rotation produces electric current.

gears

copper wire

generator

shaft

magnet

READING VISUALS What function does the magnet in the generator serve?

Direct and Alternating Currents

Think about how current flows in all of the circuits that you have studied so far. Electrons flow from one end of a battery or generator, through the circuit, and eventually back to the battery or generator. Electrons that flow in one direction produce one of two types of current.

- A **direct current** (DC) is electric charge that flows in one direction only. Direct current is produced by batteries and by DC generators such as the cell phone generator.

- An **alternating current** (AC) is a flow of electric charge that reverses direction at regular intervals. The current that enters your home and school is an alternating current.

CHECK YOUR READING What is the difference between direct current and alternating current?

Direct currents and alternating currents are produced by different generators. In an AC generator, the direction in which charge flows depends upon the direction in which the magnet moves in relation to the coil. Because generators use a rotating electromagnet, the poles of the electromagnet alternate between moving toward and moving away from the magnet. The result is a current that reverses with each half-rotation of the coil.

commutator

coil of wire

magnet

DC generator

The illustration on the right shows a simple DC generator. DC generators are very similar to AC generators. The main difference is that DC generators have a commutator that causes the current to flow in only one direction.

Many things in your home can work with either direct or alternating currents. In light bulbs, for instance, the resistance to motion of the electrons in the filament makes the filament glow. It doesn't matter in which direction the current is moving.

Some appliances can use only direct current. The black box that is on the plug of some devices is an AC–DC converter. AC–DC converters change the alternating current to direct current. For example, laptop computers use converters like the one shown in the photograph on the right. In a desktop computer, the converter is part of the power supply unit.

INVESTIGATE Electric Current

How can you identify the current?

PROCEDURE

1. Wrap the wire tightly around the middle of the compass 10–15 times. Leave about 30 cm of wire free at each end. Tape the wire to the back of the compass to keep it in place.

2. Sand the ends of the wire with sandpaper to expose about 2 cm of copper on each end. Arrange the compass on your desk so that the needle is parallel to, or lined up with, the coil. This will serve as your current detector.

3. Tape one end of the wire to one terminal of the battery. Touch the other end of the wire to the other battery terminal. Record your observations.

4. Observe the current detector as you tap the end of the wire to the battery terminal at a steady pace. Speed up or slow down your tapping until the needle of the compass alternates back and forth. Record your observations.

WHAT DO YOU THINK?

- What did you observe?
- What type of current did you detect in step 3? in step 4? How did you identify the type of current?

CHALLENGE How is this setup similar to an AC generator?

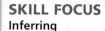

SKILL FOCUS
Inferring

MATERIALS
- piece of wire
- compass
- ruler
- tape
- sandpaper
- D cell (battery)

TIME
15 minutes

The energy that powers a car comes from burning gasoline, but the car also contains many devices that use electrical energy. Some of them are familiar—the headlights, turn signals, radio, power windows, and door locks. Others may be less familiar, such as the spark plugs that ignite the gasoline, the fuel and oil pumps that move fluids in the engine, and the air conditioner.

A car's engine includes a generator to provide current to its electrical devices. As the engine runs, it converts gasoline to kinetic energy. Some of that energy is transferred to the generator by a belt attached to its shaft. Inside the generator, a complex coil of copper wires turns in a magnetic field, generating a current that operates the electrical devices of the car.

The generator also recharges the battery, so that power is available when the engine is not running. Because the generator in most cars supplies alternating current, a car generator is usually called an alternator.

 CHECK YOUR READING What function does a generator in a car serve?

Magnets are used to control voltage.

A **transformer** is a device that increases or decreases voltage. Transformers use magnetism to control the amount of voltage. A transformer consists of two coils of wire that are wrapped around an iron ring.

An alternating current from the voltage source in the first coil produces a magnetic field. The iron ring becomes an electromagnet. Because the current alternates, the magnetic field is constantly changing. The second coil is therefore within a changing magnetic field. Current is generated in the second coil. If the two coils have the same number of loops, the voltage in the second coil will be the same as the voltage in the first coil.

A change in the voltage is caused when the two coils have different numbers of loops. If the second coil has fewer loops than the first, as in the illustration, the voltage is decreased. This is called a step-down transformer. On the other hand, if the second coil has more loops than the first, the voltage in the second circuit will be higher than the original voltage. This transformer is called a step-up transformer.

Step-Down Transformer

iron ring
coil of wire

Transformers are used in the distribution of current. Current is sent over power lines from power plants at a very high voltage. Step-down transformers on utility poles, such as the one pictured on the right, reduce the voltage available for use in homes. Sending current at high voltages minimizes the amount of energy lost to resistance along the way.

3.3 Review

KEY CONCEPTS

1. What is necessary for a magnetic field to produce an electric current?

2. Explain how electric generators convert kinetic energy into electrical energy.

3. Compare and contrast the ways in which direct current and alternating current are generated.

CRITICAL THINKING

4. **Apply** Many radios can be operated either by plugging them into the wall or by using batteries. How can a radio use either source of current?

5. **Draw Conclusions** Suppose that all of the electrical devices in a car stop working. Explain what the problem might be.

⚠ CHALLENGE

6. **Apply** European power companies deliver current at 220 V. Draw the design for a step-down transformer that would let you operate a CD player made to work at 110 V in France.

CHAPTER INVESTIGATION

Build a Speaker

OVERVIEW AND PURPOSE Speakers are found on TVs, computers, telephones, stereos, amplifiers, and other devices. Inside a speaker, magnetism and electric current interact to produce sound. The current produces a magnetic field that acts on another magnet and causes vibrations. The vibrations produce sound waves. In this lab, you will
- construct a speaker
- determine how the strength of the magnet affects the speaker's volume

▶ Problem

Write It Up

How does the strength of the magnet used to make a speaker affect the loudness of sound produced by the speaker?

▶ Hypothesize

Write It Up

Write a hypothesis that explains how you expect the strength of a magnet to affect the loudness of sound produced by the speaker, and why. Your hypothesis should be in the form of an "if . . . , then . . . , because . . . " statement.

▶ Procedure

MATERIALS
- 3 magnets of different strengths
- paper clip
- ruler
- piece of wire
- marker
- cup
- masking tape
- 2 wire leads with alligator clips
- stereo system

1. Make a data table similar to the one shown on the sample notebook page.

2. Test the strength of each magnet by measuring the distance at which a paper clip will move to the magnet, as shown. Record the measurements in your **Science Notebook.**

step 2

3. Starting about 6 cm from the end of the wire, wrap the wire around the marker 50 times to make a coil.

4. Carefully slide the coil off the marker. Wrap the ends of the wire around the coil to keep it in the shape of a circle, as shown.

step 4

5. Place the cup upside-down on your table. Tape the coil to the bottom of the cup. Clip the leads to the ends of the wire. Tape the alligator clips to the sides of the cup, as shown.

coil

step 5

6. Take turns attaching the alligator clips to the stereo as instructed by your teacher. Place each magnet on the table near the stereo. Test the speaker by holding the cup directly over each magnet and listening. Record your observations.

▶ Observe and Analyze

Write It Up

1. **RECORD OBSERVATIONS** Be sure to record your observations in the data table.

2. **INFER** Why is the coil of wire held near the magnet?

3. **APPLY** The diaphragm on a speaker vibrates to produce sound. What part of your stereo is the diaphragm?

4. **IDENTIFY** What was the independent variable in this experiment? What was the dependent variable?

▶ Conclude

Write It Up

1. **INTERPRET** Which magnet produced the loudest noise when used with your speaker? Answer the question posed in the problem.

2. **ANALYZE** Compare your results with your hypothesis. Did your results support your hypothesis?

3. **IDENTIFY LIMITS** Describe possible limitations or sources of error in the procedure or any places where errors might have occurred.

4. **APPLY** You have built a simple version of a real speaker. Apply what you have learned in this lab to explain how a real speaker might work.

▶ INVESTIGATE Further

CHALLENGE In what ways might you vary the design of the speaker to improve its functioning? Review the procedure to identify variables that might be changed to improve the speaker. Choose one variable and design an experiment to test that variable.

Build a Speaker

Problem How does the strength of the magnet used to make a speaker affect the loudness of sound produced by the speaker?

Hypothesize

Observe and Analyze

Table 1. Strength of Magnet and Loudness of Sound

Magnet	Strength (paper clip distance)	Observations
1		
2		
3		

Conclude

3.4

Generators supply electrical energy.

BEFORE, you learned

- Magnetism is a force exerted by magnets
- A moving magnetic field can generate an electric current in a conductor
- Generators use magnetism to produce current

NOW, you will learn

- How power plants generate electrical energy
- How electric power is measured
- How energy usage is calculated

VOCABULARY

electric power p. 102
watt p. 104
kilowatt p. 104
kilowatt-hour p. 105

THINK ABOUT

How can falling water generate electrical energy?

This photograph shows the Hoover Dam on the Nevada/Arizona border, which holds back a large lake, almost 600 feet deep, on the Colorado River. It took thousands of workers nearly five years to build the dam, and it cost millions of dollars. One of the main purposes of the Hoover Dam is the generation of current. Think about what you have read about generators. How could the energy of falling water be used to generate current?

Generators provide most of the world's electrical energy.

The tremendous energy produced by falling water provides the turning motion for large generators at a power plant. The power plant at the Hoover Dam supplies energy to more than a million people.

Other sources of energy at power plants include steam from burning fossil fuels, nuclear reactions, wind, solar heating, and ocean tides. Each source provides the energy of motion to the generators, producing electrical energy. **Electric power** is the rate at which electrical energy is generated from another source of energy.

VOCABULARY
Use a description wheel to take notes about *electrical power.*

CHECK YOUR READING   What do power plants that use water, steam, and wind all have in common?

How does the power plant convert the energy of motion into electrical energy? Very large generators in the plant hold powerful electromagnets surrounded by massive coils of copper wire. The illustration below shows how the energy from water falling from the reservoir to the river far below a dam is converted to electrical energy.

RESOURCE CENTER
CLASSZONE.COM

Find out more about dams that generate current.

1 As the water falls from the reservoir, its kinetic energy increases and it flows very fast. The falling stream of water turns a fan-like device, called a turbine, which is connected to the generator's shaft.

2 The rotation of the shaft turns powerful electromagnets that are surrounded by the coil of copper wires. The coil is connected to a step-up transformer that sends high-voltage current to power lines.

3 Far from the plant, step-down transformers reduce the voltage so that current can be sent through smaller lines to neighborhoods. Another transformer reduces the voltage to the level needed to operate lights and appliances.

How Electrical Power Is Generated

Power plants use generators to convert kinetic energy into electrical energy.

step-up transformers

step-down transformers

shaft

turbine

1 **Falling water** provides energy to turn the turbine of the generator.

2 The **shaft** turns a powerful electromagnet within a coil of wire, generating electrical current.

3 Current is sent along power lines at a high voltage. The voltage level is adjusted by transformers.

READING VISUALS How is kinetic energy turned into electrical energy in a power plant?

Electric power can be measured.

You have read that electric power is the rate at which electrical energy is generated from another source of energy. Power also refers to the rate at which an appliance converts electrical energy back into another form of energy, such as light, heat, or sound.

In order to provide electrical energy to homes and factories, power companies need to know the rate at which energy is needed. Power can be measured so that companies can determine how much energy is used and where it is used. This information is used to figure out how much to charge customers, and it is used to determine whether more electrical energy needs to be generated. To provide energy to an average home, a power plant needs to burn about four tons of coal each year.

RESOURCE CENTER
CLASSZONE.COM

Learn more about energy use and conservation.

Watts and Kilowatts

The unit of measurement for power is the **watt** (W). Watts measure the rate at which energy is used by an electrical appliance. For instance, a light bulb converts energy to light and heat. The power rating of the bulb, or of any device that consumes electrical energy, depends on both the voltage and the current. The formula for finding power, in watts, from voltage and current, is shown below. The letter I stands for current.

$$\textbf{Electric Power} = \textbf{Voltage} \cdot \textbf{Current}$$
$$P = VI$$

You have probably seen the label on a light bulb that gives its power rating in watts—usually in the range of 40 W to 100 W. A brighter bulb converts energy at a higher rate than one with a lower power rating.

The chart at the left shows typical power ratings, in watts, for some appliances that you might have in your home. The exact power rating depends on how each brand of appliance uses energy. You can find the actual power rating for an appliance on its label.

The combined power rating in a building is likely to be a fairly large number. A **kilowatt** (kW) is a unit of power equal to one thousand watts. All of the appliances in a room may have a combined power rating of several kilowatts, but all appliances are not in use all of the time. That is why energy is usually calculated based on how long the appliances are in use.

Typical Power Ratings	
Appliance	**Watts**
DVD player	20
Radio	20
Video game system	25
Electric blanket	60
Light bulb	75
Stereo system	100
Window fan	100
Television	110
Computer	120
Computer monitor	150
Refrigerator	700
Air conditioner	1000
Microwave oven	1000
Hair dryer	1200
Clothes dryer	3000

CHECK YOUR READING Explain what kilowatts are used to measure.

INVESTIGATE Power

How would you use your electrical energy?

PROCEDURE

① On a sheet of graph paper, outline a box that is 10 squares long by 18 squares wide. The box represents a room that is wired to power a total of 1800 W. Each square represents 10 W of power.

② From the chart on page 104, choose appliances that you want in your room. Using colored pencils, fill in the appropriate number of boxes for each appliance.

③ All of the items that you choose must fit within the total power available, represented by the 180 squares.

WHAT DO YOU THINK?

• How did you decide to use your electrical energy?

• Could you provide enough energy to operate everything you wanted at one time?

CHALLENGE During the summer, power companies sometimes cannot produce enough energy for the demand. Why do you think that happens?

SKILL FOCUS
Making models

MATERIALS
• graph paper
• colored pencils

TIME

30 minutes

Calculating Energy Use

The electric bill for your energy usage is calculated based on the rate at which energy is used, or the power, and the amount of time it is used at that rate. Total energy used by an appliance is determined by multiplying its power consumption by the amount of time that it is used.

$$\text{Energy used} = \text{Power} \cdot \text{time}$$

$$E = Pt$$

The kilowatt-hour is the unit of measurement for energy usage. A **kilowatt-hour** (kWh) is equal to one kilowatt of power for a one-hour period. Buildings usually have meters that measure how many kilowatt-hours of energy have been used. The meters display four or five small dials in a row, as shown in the photograph on the right. Each dial represents a different place value—ones, tens, hundreds, or thousands. For example, the meter in the photograph shows that the customer has used close to 9000 kWh of energy—8933 kWh, to be exact. To find how much energy was used in one month, the last month's reading is subtracted from this total.

To determine the number of kilowatt-hours of energy used by an appliance, find its wattage on the chart on page 104 or from the label. Then, substitute it into the formula along with the number of hours it was in use. Solve the sample problems below.

Finding Energy Used

Sample Problem

How much energy is used to dry clothes in a 3 kW dryer for 30 minutes?

What do you know?	Power = 3.0 kW, time = 0.5 hr
What do you want to find out?	Energy used
Write the formula:	$E = Pt$
Substitute into the formula:	$E = 3.0 \text{ kW} \cdot 0.5 \text{ hr}$
Calculate and simplify:	$E = 1.5 \text{ kWh}$
Check that your units agree:	Unit is kWh. Unit for energy used is kWh. Units agree.
Answer:	1.5 kWh

Practice the Math

1. All of the appliances in a computer lab are in use for 6 hours every day and together use 3.3 kW. How much energy has been used in 1 day?
2. How much energy is used when a 1.2 kW hair dyer is in use for 0.2 hr?

Energy prices vary, but you can estimate the cost of using an electrical appliance by using a value of about 10–12 cents/kWh. You can calculate how much energy you can save by turning off the lights or television when you are not using them. Although the number may seem small, try multiplying your savings over the course of a month or year.

3.4 Review

KEY CONCEPTS

1. How do power plants generate electrical energy from kinetic energy?
2. Explain what watts measure.
3. How is energy use determined?

CRITICAL THINKING

4. **Apply** Think about reducing energy usage in your home. What changes would make the largest difference in the amount of energy used?

5. **Calculate** How much energy is used if a 3000 W clothes dryer is used for 4 hours?

⬤ CHALLENGE

6. **Calculate** An electric bill for an apartment shows 396 kWh of energy used over one month. The appliances in the apartment have a total power rating of 2.2 kW. How many hours were the appliances in use?

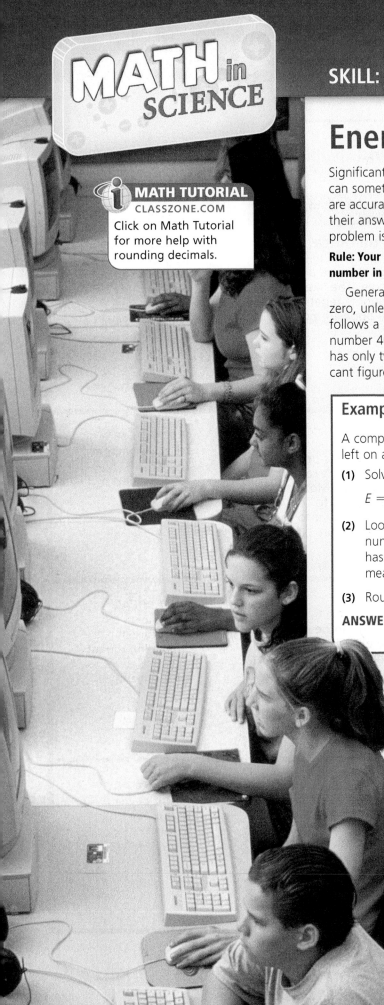

MATH TUTORIAL
CLASSZONE.COM
Click on Math Tutorial for more help with rounding decimals.

Energy Calculations

Significant figures are meaningful digits in a number. Calculations can sometimes produce answers with more significant figures than are accurately known. Scientists use rules to determine how to round their answers. The rule for writing an answer to a multiplication problem is shown below.

Rule: Your answer may show only as many significant figures as the number in the problem with the fewest significant figures.

Generally, a significant figure is any digit shown except for a zero, unless the zero is contained between two nonzero digits or follows a nonzero digit after a decimal point. For example, the number 40.3 has three significant figures, but the number 0.90 has only two significant figures. The number 0.034 has two significant figures, and the number 0.8 has only one significant figure.

Example

A computer uses 6.5 kWh of energy per day. If the computer is left on all the time, how much energy does it use in a year?

(1) Solve the problem.

$$E = 6.5 \; \frac{\text{kWh}}{\text{day}} \cdot 365 \; \frac{\text{days}}{\text{year}} = 2372.5 \; \frac{\text{kWh}}{\text{year}}$$

(2) Look at the number with the fewest significant figures. The number 6.5 has two significant figures, and the number 365 has three significant figures. Therefore, the answer is only meaningful to two significant figures.

(3) Round the answer to two significant figures.

ANSWER $E = 2400 \; \frac{\text{kWh}}{\text{year}}$

Answer the following questions. Write your answers using the significant figure rule for multiplication.

1. How much energy is used in a year by a computer that uses 1.7 kWh/day?

2. An energy-efficient computer uses 0.72 kWh/day. How much energy does it use in a week?

3. How much energy is used in one year if a 0.27 kW computer is on for 3 hours/day? (**Hint:** Use the formula $E = Pt$.)

CHALLENGE The energy usage of a computer is measured to be 0.058030 kWh. How many significant figures does this measurement have?

3 Chapter Review

the BIG idea

Current can produce magnetism, and magnetism can produce current.

CONTENT REVIEW
CLASSZONE.COM

KEY CONCEPTS SUMMARY

3.1) Magnetism is a force that acts at a distance.

magnetic poles

magnetic field lines

Opposite poles attract.

All magnets have a north and south pole. The like poles of two magnets repel each other and the opposite poles attract.

VOCABULARY
magnet p. 79
magnetism p. 80
magnetic pole p. 80
magnetic field p. 81
magnetic domain p. 82

3.2) Current can produce magnetism.

motor

magnet

electromagnet

A magnet that is produced by electric current is called an electromagnet. Motors use electromagnets to convert electrical energy into the energy of motion.

VOCABULARY
electromagnetism p. 89
electromagnet p. 90

3.3) Magnetism can produce current.

generator

magnet

electromagnet

Magnetism can be used to produce electric current. In a generator the energy of motion is converted into electrical energy.

VOCABULARY
generator p. 96
direct current p. 97
alternating current p. 97
transformer p. 99

3.4) Generators supply electrical energy.

generator

shaft

turbine

Generators at power plants use large magnets to produce electric current, supplying electrical energy to homes and businesses.

VOCABULARY
electric power p. 102
watt p. 104
kilowatt p. 104
kilowatt-hour p. 105

Reviewing Vocabulary

Draw a cluster diagram for each of the terms below. Write the vocabulary term in the center circle. In another circle, write the definition of the term in your own words. Add other circles that give examples or characteristics of the term. A sample diagram is completed for you.

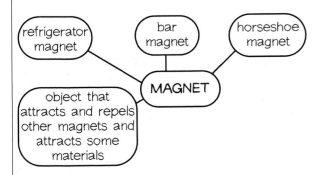

1. magnetism
2. magnetic pole
3. magnetic field
4. magnetic domain
5. electromagnet
6. generator
7. direct current
8. alternating current
9. transformer
10. electric power
11. watt
12. kilowatt-hour

Reviewing Key Concepts

Multiple Choice *Choose the letter of the best answer.*

13. Magnetic field lines flow from a magnet's
    a. north pole to south pole
    b. south pole to north pole
    c. center to the outside
    d. outside to the center

14. Which of the following is characteristic of magnetic materials?
    a. Their atoms are all aligned.
    b. Their atoms are arranged in magnetic domains.
    c. They are all nonmetals.
    d. They are all made of lodestone.

15. The Earth's magnetic field helps to protect living things from
    a. ultraviolet light
    b. meteors
    c. the Northern Lights
    d. charged particles

16. To produce a magnetic field around a copper wire, you have to
    a. place it in Earth's magnetic field
    b. run a current through it
    c. supply kinetic energy to it
    d. place it near a strong magnet

17. An electric current is produced when a wire is
    a. stationary in a magnetic field
    b. moving in a magnetic field
    c. placed between the poles of a magnet
    d. coiled around a magnet

18. In a generator, kinetic energy is converted into
    a. light energy
    b. chemical energy
    c. electrical energy
    d. nuclear energy

19. In an AC circuit, the current moves
    a. back and forth
    b. from one end of a generator to the other
    c. from one end of a battery to the other
    d. in one direction

20. What is the function of the turbine in a power plant?
    a. to increase the voltage
    b. to convert DC to AC
    c. to cool the steam
    d. to turn the coil or magnet

21. The two factors needed to measure usage of electrical energy in a building are
    a. power and time
    b. power and voltage
    c. voltage and time
    d. current and voltage

iron strip

iron core

copper wire

Refer to the device in the illustration above to answer the next three questions.

22. APPLY What will happen when the switch is closed?

23. PREDICT What effect will switching the direction of the current have on the operation of the device?

24. CONTRAST If the iron strip is replaced with a thin magnet, how would that affect the answers to the previous two questions?

25. APPLY Coal is burned at a power plant to produce steam. The rising steam turns a turbine. Describe how the motion of the turbine produces current at the plant.

26. CONNECT List three things that you use in your everyday life that would not exist without the discovery of electromagnetism.

27. APPLY A radio for use during power outages works when you crank a handle. How is the radio powered? How can it keep operating even after you stop turning the crank?

28. HYPOTHESIZE Use your understanding of magnetic materials and the source of Earth's magnetic field to form a hypothesis about the difference between Earth and the Moon that accounts for the fact that the Moon does not have a magnetic field.

Some electric bills include a bar graph of energy usage similar to the one shown below. Use the information provided in the graph to answer the next four questions.

12-Month Usage (kWh)

months billed

29. The first bar in the graph shows energy usage for the month of January. About how much energy, in kWh, was used in January?

30. If the appliances in the building have a combined power rating of 2 kW, how many hours were they in use during the month of March? (**Hint:** Use the formula $E = Pt$.)

31. The cost of energy was 8 cents per kWh. How much was charged for energy usage in May?

32. The most energy is used when the air conditioner is on. During which three months was the air conditioner on?

the BIG idea

33. ANALYZE Look back at pages 76–77. Think about the answer you gave to the question about the large photograph. How has your understanding of magnetism changed? Give examples.

34. SUMMARIZE Write a paragraph summarizing the first three pages of this chapter. Use the heading at the top of page 79 as your topic sentence. Explain each red and blue heading.

UNIT PROJECTS

Evaluate all the data, results, and information from your project folder. Prepare to present your project.

For practice on your
state test, go to . . .
i **TEST PRACTICE**
CLASSZONE.COM

Analyzing Tables

The table below lists some major advances in the understanding of electromagnetism.

Scientist	Year	Advance
William Gilbert	1600	proposes distinction between magnetism and static electricity
Pieter van Musschenbroek	1745	develops Leyden jar, which stores electric charge
Benjamin Franklin	1752	shows that lightning is a form of electricity
Charles Augustin de Coulomb	1785	proves mathematically that, for electricity and magnetism, force changes with distance
Alessandro Volta	1800	invents battery, first device to generate a continuous current
Hans Christian Oersted	1820	announces he had used electric current to produce magnetic effects
André Marie Ampère	1820	shows that wires carrying current attract and repel each other, just like magnets
Georg Simon Ohm	1827	studies how well different wires conduct electric current
Michael Faraday	1831	produces electricity with a magnet; invents first electric generator

Use the table above to answer the next four questions.

1. Which scientist first produced a device that allowed experimenters to hold an electric charge for later use?
  a. Coulomb   **c.** Ohm
  b. Franklin   **d.** van Musschenbroek

2. Which scientist developed the first device that could be used to provide a steady source of current to other devices?
  a. Ampère   **c.** Volta
  b. Faraday   **d.** Gilbert

3. Which scientist had the first experimental evidence that current could produce magnetism?
  a. Gilbert   **c.** van Musschenbroek
  b. Faraday   **d.** Oersted

4. Why was Coulomb's work important?
  a. He showed that electricity and magnetism could be stored.
  b. He showed that electricity and magnetism behave similarly.
  c. He proved that electricity and magnetism were different.
  d. He proved that electricity and magnetism were the same.

Extended Response

Answer the two questions below in detail. Include some of the terms from the word box. Underline each term you use in your answer.

appliance	current	generator
motor	coil	kilowatt-hour

5. How are electromagnets produced? How can the strength of these devices be increased? How can electromagnets be used in ways that permanent magnets cannot?

6. Alix chats online for an average of about an hour a day 6 days a week. Her computer has a power rating of 270 watts. She has a hair dryer with a power rating of 1200 watts. She uses it twice a week for about 15 minutes at a time. Which device is likely to use more power over the course of a year? Why?

Today's Scientist at Work

Name: Mark Dean	
Degree: PhD, Electrical Engineering, Stanford University	
Profession: Electrical Engineer, Computer Researcher	
Location: San Jose, California	

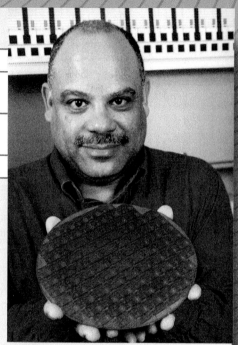

IBM/AP Photo

Dr. Mark Dean has a very confident view of the future of computer technology. "If you can talk about it, that means it's possible," he says. Dr. Dean played an important role in bringing desktop computers into the home. Among other things, Dr. Dean devised the circuits used in early personal computers to connect to printers and modems.

Dr. Dean has designed computers since the early days of the personal computer. He led a team of engineers that made the first 1-gigahertz computer chip. The chip could do a billion calculations per second. He also was involved in designing the world's most powerful supercomputer systems, which can make trillions of calculations per second. One of the improvements IBM researchers are working on now is creating chips that use less energy. He once joked that "if we don't solve this problem, some products could be used for cooking as well as computing."

A dust-free environment is required to manufacture computer chips.

© John Madere/Corbis

Today, Dr. Dean is leading a research lab of several hundred scientists. They are creating a wide range of future computer technologies. These range from low-power circuits, to powerful and easy-to-use software. They also work on new ways to use computers to improve our lives and businesses. He would tell any student today that "if you work hard, you can be whatever you want to be. There may be obstacles, but there are no limits."

Student Resource Handbooks

Scientific Thinking Handbook

Making Observations

An **observation** is an act of noting and recording an event, characteristic, behavior, or anything else detected with an instrument or with the senses.

Observations allow you to make informed hypotheses and to gather data for experiments. Careful observations often lead to ideas for new experiments. There are two categories of observations:

- **Quantitative observations** can be expressed in numbers and include records of time, temperature, mass, distance, and volume.

- **Qualitative observations** include descriptions of sights, sounds, smells, and textures.

EXAMPLE

A student dissolved 30 grams of Epsom salts in water, poured the solution into a dish, and let the dish sit out uncovered overnight. The next day, she made the following observations of the Epsom salt crystals that grew in the dish.

Table 1. Observations of Epsom Salt Crystals

To determine the mass, the student found the mass of the dish before and after growing the crystals and then used subtraction to find the difference.

The student measured several crystals and calculated the mean length. (To learn how to calculate the mean of a data set, see page R36.)

Quantitative Observations	Qualitative Observations
• mass = 30 g • mean crystal length = 0.5 cm • longest crystal length = 2 cm	• Crystals are clear. • Crystals are long, thin, and rectangular. • White crust has formed around edge of dish.

Photographs or sketches are useful for recording qualitative observations.

Epsom salt crystals

MORE ABOUT OBSERVING

- Make quantitative observations whenever possible. That way, others will know exactly what you observed and be able to compare their results with yours.

- It is always a good idea to make qualitative observations too. You never know when you might observe something unexpected.

Predicting and Hypothesizing

A **prediction** is an expectation of what will be observed or what will happen. A **hypothesis** is a tentative explanation for an observation or scientific problem that can be tested by further investigation.

EXAMPLE

Suppose you have made two paper airplanes and you wonder why one of them tends to glide farther than the other one.

1. Start by asking a question.

2. Make an educated guess. After examination, you notice that the wings of the airplane that flies farther are slightly larger than the wings of the other airplane.

3. Write a prediction based upon your educated guess, in the form of an "If . . . , then . . ." statement. Write the independent variable after the word *if,* and the dependent variable after the word *then.*

4. To make a hypothesis, explain why you think what you predicted will occur. Write the explanation after the word *because.*

1. Why does one of the paper airplanes glide farther than the other?

2. The size of an airplane's wings may affect how far the airplane will glide.

3. Prediction: If I make a paper airplane with larger wings, then the airplane will glide farther.

To read about independent and dependent variables, see page R30.

4. Hypothesis: If I make a paper airplane with larger wings, then the airplane will glide farther, because the additional surface area of the wing will produce more lift.

Notice that the part of the hypothesis after *because* adds an explanation of why the airplane will glide farther.

MORE ABOUT HYPOTHESES

- The results of an experiment cannot prove that a hypothesis is correct. Rather, the results either support or do not support the hypothesis.

- Valuable information is gained even when your hypothesis is not supported by your results. For example, it would be an important discovery to find that wing size is not related to how far an airplane glides.

- In science, a hypothesis is supported only after many scientists have conducted many experiments and produced consistent results.

Inferring

An **inference** is a logical conclusion drawn from the available evidence and prior knowledge. Inferences are often made from observations.

EXAMPLE

A student observing a set of acorns noticed something unexpected about one of them. He noticed a white, soft-bodied insect eating its way out of the acorn.

The student recorded these observations.

Observations

- There is a hole in the acorn, about 0.5 cm in diameter, where the insect crawled out.
- There is a second hole, which is about the size of a pinhole, on the other side of the acorn.
- The inside of the acorn is hollow.

Here are some inferences that can be made on the basis of the observations.

Inferences

- The insect formed from the material inside the acorn, grew to its present size, and ate its way out of the acorn.
- The insect crawled through the smaller hole, ate the inside of the acorn, grew to its present size, and ate its way out of the acorn.
- An egg was laid in the acorn through the smaller hole. The egg hatched into a larva that ate the inside of the acorn, grew to its present size, and ate its way out of the acorn.

When you make inferences, be sure to look at all of the evidence available and combine it with what you already know.

MORE ABOUT INFERENCES

Inferences depend both on observations and on the knowledge of the people making the inferences. Ancient people who did not know that organisms are produced only by similar organisms might have made an inference like the first one. A student today might look at the same observations and make the second inference. A third student might have knowledge about this particular insect and know that it is never small enough to fit through the smaller hole, leading her to the third inference.

Identifying Cause and Effect

In a **cause-and-effect relationship,** one event or characteristic is the result of another. Usually an effect follows its cause in time.

There are many examples of cause-and-effect relationships in everyday life.

Cause	Effect
Turn off a light.	Room gets dark.
Drop a glass.	Glass breaks.
Blow a whistle.	Sound is heard.

Scientists must be careful not to infer a cause-and-effect relationship just because one event happens after another event. When one event occurs after another, you cannot infer a cause-and-effect relationship on the basis of that information alone. You also cannot conclude that one event caused another if there are alternative ways to explain the second event. A scientist must demonstrate through experimentation or continued observation that an event was truly caused by another event.

EXAMPLE

Make an Observation

Suppose you have a few plants growing outside. When the weather starts getting colder, you bring one of the plants indoors. You notice that the plant you brought indoors is growing faster than the others are growing. You cannot conclude from your observation that the change in temperature was the cause of the increased plant growth, because there are alternative explanations for the observation. Some possible explanations are given below.

- The humidity indoors caused the plant to grow faster.

- The level of sunlight indoors caused the plant to grow faster.

- The indoor plant's being noticed more often and watered more often than the outdoor plants caused it to grow faster.

- The plant that was brought indoors was healthier than the other plants to begin with.

To determine which of these factors, if any, caused the indoor plant to grow faster than the outdoor plants, you would need to design and conduct an experiment.

See pages R28–R35 for information about designing experiments.

Recognizing Bias

Television, newspapers, and the Internet are full of experts claiming to have scientific evidence to back up their claims. How do you know whether the claims are really backed up by good science?

Bias is a slanted point of view, or personal prejudice. The goal of scientists is to be as objective as possible and to base their findings on facts instead of opinions. However, bias often affects the conclusions of researchers, and it is important to learn to recognize bias.

When scientific results are reported, you should consider the source of the information as well as the information itself. It is important to critically analyze the information that you see and read.

SOURCES OF BIAS

There are several ways in which a report of scientific information may be biased. Here are some questions that you can ask yourself:

1. **Who is sponsoring the research?**

   Sometimes, the results of an investigation are biased because an organization paying for the research is looking for a specific answer. This type of bias can affect how data are gathered and interpreted.

2. **Is the research sample large enough?**

   Sometimes research does not include enough data. The larger the sample size, the more likely that the results are accurate, assuming a truly random sample.

3. **In a survey, who is answering the questions?**

   The results of a survey or poll can be biased. The people taking part in the survey may have been specifically chosen because of how they would answer. They may have the same ideas or lifestyles. A survey or poll should make use of a random sample of people.

4. **Are the people who take part in a survey biased?**

   People who take part in surveys sometimes try to answer the questions the way they think the researcher wants them to answer. Also, in surveys or polls that ask for personal information, people may be unwilling to answer questions truthfully.

SCIENTIFIC BIAS

It is also important to realize that scientists have their own biases because of the types of research they do and because of their scientific viewpoints. Two scientists may look at the same set of data and come to completely different conclusions because of these biases. However, such disagreements are not necessarily bad. In fact, a critical analysis of disagreements is often responsible for moving science forward.

Identifying Faulty Reasoning

Faulty reasoning is wrong or incorrect thinking. It leads to mistakes and to wrong conclusions. Scientists are careful not to draw unreasonable conclusions from experimental data. Without such caution, the results of scientific investigations may be misleading.

EXAMPLE

Scientists try to make generalizations based on their data to explain as much about nature as possible. If only a small sample of data is looked at, however, a conclusion may be faulty. Suppose a scientist has studied the effects of the El Niño and La Niña weather patterns on flood damage in California from 1989 to 1995. The scientist organized the data in the bar graph below.

The scientist drew the following conclusions:

1. The La Niña weather pattern has no effect on flooding in California.
2. When neither weather pattern occurs, there is almost no flood damage.
3. A weak or moderate El Niño produces a small or moderate amount of flooding.
4. A strong El Niño produces a lot of flooding.

Flood and Storm Damage in California

Estimated damage (millions of dollars)

Legend: Weak–moderate El Niño, Strong El Niño

Starting year of season (July 1–June 30)

SOURCE: *Governor's Office of Emergency Services, California*

For the six-year period of the scientist's investigation, these conclusions may seem to be reasonable. However, a six-year study of weather patterns may be too small of a sample for the conclusions to be supported. Consider the following graph, which shows information that was gathered from 1949 to 1997.

Flood and Storm Damage in California from 1949 to 1997

Estimated damage (millions of dollars)

Weak–moderate El Niño   Weak–moderate La Niña   **Starting year of season**
Strong El Niño   Strong La Niña   **(July 1–June 30)**
Neither

SOURCE: *Governor's Office of Emergency Services, California*

The only one of the conclusions that all of this information supports is number 3: a weak or moderate El Niño produces a small or moderate amount of flooding. By collecting more data, scientists can be more certain of their conclusions and can avoid faulty reasoning.

Analyzing Statements

To **analyze** a statement is to examine its parts carefully. Scientific findings are often reported through media such as television or the Internet. A report that is made public often focuses on only a small part of research. As a result, it is important to question the sources of information.

Evaluate Media Claims

To **evaluate** a statement is to judge it on the basis of criteria you've established. Sometimes evaluating means deciding whether a statement is true.

Reports of scientific research and findings in the media may be misleading or incomplete. When you are exposed to this information, you should ask yourself some questions so that you can make informed judgments about the information.

1. Does the information come from a credible source?

Suppose you learn about a new product and it is stated that scientific evidence proves that the product works. A report from a respected news source may be more believable than an advertisement paid for by the product's manufacturer.

2. How much evidence supports the claim?

Often, it may seem that there is new evidence every day of something in the world that either causes or cures an illness. However, information that is the result of several years of work by several different scientists is more credible than an advertisement that does not even cite the subjects of the experiment.

3. How much information is being presented?

Science cannot solve all questions, and scientific experiments often have flaws. A report that discusses problems in a scientific study may be more believable than a report that addresses only positive experimental findings.

4. Is scientific evidence being presented by a specific source?

Sometimes scientific findings are reported by people who are called experts or leaders in a scientific field. But if their names are not given or their scientific credentials are not reported, their statements may be less credible than those of recognized experts.

Differentiate Between Fact and Opinion

Sometimes information is presented as a fact when it may be an opinion. When scientific conclusions are reported, it is important to recognize whether they are based on solid evidence. Again, you may find it helpful to ask yourself some questions.

1. **What is the difference between a fact and an opinion?**

   A **fact** is a piece of information that can be strictly defined and proved true. An **opinion** is a statement that expresses a belief, value, or feeling. An opinion cannot be proved true or false. For example, a person's age is a fact, but if someone is asked how old they feel, it is impossible to prove the person's answer to be true or false.

2. **Can opinions be measured?**

   Yes, opinions can be measured. In fact, surveys often ask for people's opinions on a topic. But there is no way to know whether or not an opinion is the truth.

HOW TO DIFFERENTIATE FACT FROM OPINION

Human Activities and the Environment

Opinions
Notice words or phrases that express beliefs or feelings. The words *unfortunately* and *careless* show that opinions are being expressed.

Unfortunately, human use of fossil fuels is one of the most significant developments of the past few centuries. Humans rely on fossil fuels, a non-renewable energy resource, for more than 90 percent of their energy needs.

Facts
Statements that contain statistics tend to be facts. Writers often use facts to support their opinions.

Opinion
Look for statements that speculate about events. These statements are opinions, because they cannot be proved.

This careless misuse of our planet's resources has resulted in pollution, global warming, and the destruction of fragile ecosystems. For example, oil pipelines carry more than one million barrels of oil each day across tundra regions. Transporting oil across such areas can only result in oil spills that poison the land for decades.

Lab Handbook

Safety Rules

Before you work in the laboratory, read these safety rules twice. Ask your teacher to explain any rules that you do not completely understand. Refer to these rules later on if you have questions about safety in the science classroom.

Directions

- Read all directions and make sure that you understand them before starting an investigation or lab activity. If you do not understand how to do a procedure or how to use a piece of equipment, ask your teacher.
- Do not begin any investigation or touch any equipment until your teacher has told you to start.
- Never experiment on your own. If you want to try a procedure that the directions do not call for, ask your teacher for permission first.
- If you are hurt or injured in any way, tell your teacher immediately.

Dress Code

goggles

apron

gloves

- Wear goggles when
  — using glassware, sharp objects, or chemicals
  — heating an object
  — working with anything that can easily fly up into the air and hurt someone's eye
- Tie back long hair or hair that hangs in front of your eyes.
- Remove any article of clothing—such as a loose sweater or a scarf—that hangs down and may touch a flame, chemical, or piece of equipment.
- Observe all safety icons calling for the wearing of eye protection, gloves, and aprons.

Heating and Fire Safety

fire safety

heating safety

- Keep your work area neat, clean, and free of extra materials.
- Never reach over a flame or heat source.
- Point objects being heated away from you and others.
- Never heat a substance or an object in a closed container.
- Never touch an object that has been heated. If you are unsure whether something is hot, treat it as though it is. Use oven mitts, clamps, tongs, or a test-tube holder.
- Know where the fire extinguisher and fire blanket are kept in your classroom.
- Do not throw hot substances into the trash. Wait for them to cool or use the container your teacher puts out for disposal.

Electrical Safety

electrical
safety

- Never use lamps or other electrical equipment with frayed cords.
- Make sure no cord is lying on the floor where someone can trip over it.
- Do not let a cord hang over the side of a counter or table so that the equipment can easily be pulled or knocked to the floor.
- Never let cords hang into sinks or other places where water can be found.
- Never try to fix electrical problems. Inform your teacher of any problems immediately.
- Unplug an electrical cord by pulling on the plug, not the cord.

Chemical Safety

chemical
safety

poison

fumes

- If you spill a chemical or get one on your skin or in your eyes, tell your teacher right away.
- Never touch, taste, or sniff any chemicals in the lab. If you need to determine odor, waft. Wafting consists of holding the chemical in its container 15 centimeters (6 in.) away from your nose, and using your fingers to bring fumes from the container to your nose.
- Keep lids on all chemicals you are not using.
- Never put unused chemicals back into the original containers. Throw away extra chemicals where your teacher tells you to.
- Pour chemicals over a sink or your work area, not over the floor.
- If you get a chemical in your eye, use the eyewash right away.
- Always wash your hands after handling chemicals, plants, or soil.

Wafting

Glassware and Sharp-Object Safety

sharp
objects

- If you break glassware, tell your teacher right away.
- Do not use broken or chipped glassware. Give these to your teacher.
- Use knives and other cutting instruments carefully. Always wear eye protection and cut away from you.

Animal Safety

- Never hurt an animal.
- Touch animals only when necessary. Follow your teacher's instructions for handling animals.
- Always wash your hands after working with animals.

Cleanup

disposal

- Follow your teacher's instructions for throwing away or putting away supplies.
- Clean your work area and pick up anything that has dropped to the floor.
- Wash your hands.

Using Lab Equipment

Different experiments require different types of equipment. But even though experiments differ, the ways in which the equipment is used are the same.

Beakers

- Use beakers for holding and pouring liquids.

- Do not use a beaker to measure the volume of a liquid. Use a graduated cylinder instead. (See page R16.)

- Use a beaker that holds about twice as much liquid as you need. For example, if you need 100 milliliters of water, you should use a 200- or 250-milliliter beaker.

Test Tubes

- Use test tubes to hold small amounts of substances.

- Do not use a test tube to measure the volume of a liquid.

- Use a test tube when heating a substance over a flame. Aim the mouth of the tube away from yourself and other people.

- Liquids easily spill or splash from test tubes, so it is important to use only small amounts of liquids.

Test-Tube Holder

- Use a test-tube holder when heating a substance in a test tube.

- Use a test-tube holder if the substance in a test tube is dangerous to touch.

- Make sure the test-tube holder tightly grips the test tube so that the test tube will not slide out of the holder.

- Make sure that the test-tube holder is above the surface of the substance in the test tube so that you can observe the substance.

Test-Tube Rack

- Use a test-tube rack to organize test tubes before, during, and after an experiment.

- Use a test-tube rack to keep test tubes upright so that they do not fall over and spill their contents.

- Use a test-tube rack that is the correct size for the test tubes that you are using. If the rack is too small, a test tube may become stuck. If the rack is too large, a test tube may lean over, and some of its contents may spill or splash.

Forceps

- Use forceps when you need to pick up or hold a very small object that should not be touched with your hands.

- Do not use forceps to hold anything over a flame, because forceps are not long enough to keep your hand safely away from the flame. Plastic forceps will melt, and metal forceps will conduct heat and burn your hand.

Hot Plate

- Use a hot plate when a substance needs to be kept warmer than room temperature for a long period of time.

- Use a hot plate instead of a Bunsen burner or a candle when you need to carefully control temperature.

- Do not use a hot plate when a substance needs to be burned in an experiment.

- Always use "hot hands" safety mitts or oven mitts when handling anything that has been heated on a hot plate.

Microscope

Scientists use microscopes to see very small objects that cannot easily be seen with the eye alone. A microscope magnifies the image of an object so that small details may be observed. A microscope that you may use can magnify an object 400 times—the object will appear 400 times larger than its actual size.

Body The body separates the lens in the eyepiece from the objective lenses below.

Nosepiece The nosepiece holds the objective lenses above the stage and rotates so that all lenses may be used.

High-Power Objective Lens This is the largest lens on the nosepiece. It magnifies an image approximately 40 times.

Stage The stage supports the object being viewed.

Diaphragm The diaphragm is used to adjust the amount of light passing through the slide and into an objective lens.

Mirror or Light Source Some microscopes use light that is reflected through the stage by a mirror. Other microscopes have their own light sources.

Eyepiece Objects are viewed through the eyepiece. The eyepiece contains a lens that commonly magnifies an image 10 times.

Coarse Adjustment This knob is used to focus the image of an object when it is viewed through the low-power lens.

Fine Adjustment This knob is used to focus the image of an object when it is viewed through the high-power lens.

Low-Power Objective Lens This is the smallest lens on the nosepiece. It magnifies an image approximately 10 times.

Arm The arm supports the body above the stage. Always carry a microscope by the arm and base.

Stage Clip The stage clip holds a slide in place on the stage.

Base The base supports the microscope.

VIEWING AN OBJECT

1. Use the coarse adjustment knob to raise the body tube.

2. Adjust the diaphragm so that you can see a bright circle of light through the eyepiece.

3. Place the object or slide on the stage. Be sure that it is centered over the hole in the stage.

4. Turn the nosepiece to click the low-power lens into place.

5. Using the coarse adjustment knob, slowly lower the lens and focus on the specimen being viewed. Be sure not to touch the slide or object with the lens.

6. When switching from the low-power lens to the high-power lens, first raise the body tube with the coarse adjustment knob so that the high-power lens will not hit the slide.

7. Turn the nosepiece to click the high-power lens into place.

8. Use the fine adjustment knob to focus on the specimen being viewed. Again, be sure not to touch the slide or object with the lens.

MAKING A SLIDE, OR WET MOUNT

1 Place the specimen in the center of a clean slide.

2 Place a drop of water on the specimen.

3 Place a cover slip on the slide. Put one edge of the cover slip into the drop of water and slowly lower it over the specimen.

4 Remove any air bubbles from under the cover slip by gently tapping the cover slip.

5 Dry any excess water before placing the slide on the microscope stage for viewing.

Spring Scale (Force Meter)

- Use a spring scale to measure a force pulling on the scale.
- Use a spring scale to measure the force of gravity exerted on an object by Earth.
- To measure a force accurately, a spring scale must be zeroed before it is used. The scale is zeroed when no weight is attached and the indicator is positioned at zero.
- Do not attach a weight that is either too heavy or too light to a spring scale. A weight that is too heavy could break the scale or exert too great a force for the scale to measure. A weight that is too light may not exert enough force to be measured accurately.

Graduated Cylinder

- Use a graduated cylinder to measure the volume of a liquid.
- Be sure that the graduated cylinder is on a flat surface so that your measurement will be accurate.
- When reading the scale on a graduated cylinder, be sure to have your eyes at the level of the surface of the liquid.
- The surface of the liquid will be curved in the graduated cylinder. Read the volume of the liquid at the bottom of the curve, or meniscus (muh-NIHS-kuhs).
- You can use a graduated cylinder to find the volume of a solid object by measuring the increase in a liquid's level after you add the object to the cylinder.

meniscus

Read the volume at the bottom of the meniscus. The volume is 96 mL.

Metric Rulers

- Use metric rulers or meter sticks to measure objects' lengths.

- Do not measure an object from the end of a metric ruler or meter stick, because the end is often imperfect. Instead, measure from the 1-centimeter mark, but remember to subtract a centimeter from the apparent measurement.

- Estimate any lengths that extend between marked units. For example, if a meter stick shows centimeters but not millimeters, you can estimate the length that an object extends between centimeter marks to measure it to the nearest millimeter.

- **Controlling Variables** If you are taking repeated measurements, always measure from the same point each time. For example, if you're measuring how high two different balls bounce when dropped from the same height, measure both bounces at the same point on the balls—either the top or the bottom. Do not measure at the top of one ball and the bottom of the other.

EXAMPLE

How to Measure a Leaf

1. Lay a ruler flat on top of the leaf so that the 1-centimeter mark lines up with one end. Make sure the ruler and the leaf do not move between the time you line them up and the time you take the measurement.

2. Look straight down on the ruler so that you can see exactly how the marks line up with the other end of the leaf.

3. Estimate the length by which the leaf extends beyond a marking. For example, the leaf below extends about halfway between the 4.2-centimeter and 4.3-centimeter marks, so the apparent measurement is about 4.25 centimeters.

4. Remember to subtract 1 centimeter from your apparent measurement, since you started at the 1-centimeter mark on the ruler and not at the end. The leaf is about 3.25 centimeters long (4.25 cm – 1 cm = 3.25 cm).

Triple-Beam Balance

This balance has a pan and three beams with sliding masses, called riders. At one end of the beams is a pointer that indicates whether the mass on the pan is equal to the masses shown on the beams.

1. Make sure the balance is zeroed before measuring the mass of an object. The balance is zeroed if the pointer is at zero when nothing is on the pan and the riders are at their zero points. Use the adjustment knob at the base of the balance to zero it.

2. Place the object to be measured on the pan.

3. Move the riders one notch at a time away from the pan. Begin with the largest rider. If moving the largest rider one notch brings the pointer below zero, begin measuring the mass of the object with the next smaller rider.

4. Change the positions of the riders until they balance the mass on the pan and the pointer is at zero. Then add the readings from the three beams to determine the mass of the object.

300 g	position of largest rider
90 g	position of middle rider
+ 3 g	position of smallest rider
393 g	mass of beaker

pan

beams

largest rider (300 g)

middle rider (90 g)

smallest rider (3 g)

Double-Pan Balance

This type of balance has two pans. Between the pans is a pointer that indicates whether the masses on the pans are equal.

1. Make sure the balance is zeroed before measuring the mass of an object. The balance is zeroed if the pointer is at zero when there is nothing on either of the pans. Many double-pan balances have sliding knobs that can be used to zero them.

2. Place the object to be measured on one of the pans.

3. Begin adding standard masses to the other pan. Begin with the largest standard mass. If this adds too much mass to the balance, begin measuring the mass of the object with the next smaller standard mass.

4. Add standard masses until the masses on both pans are balanced and the pointer is at zero. Then add the standard masses together to determine the mass of the object being measured.

	200 g
	100 g
	50 g
	20 g
	20 g
	2 g
+	1 g

393 g mass of beaker

Never place chemicals or liquids directly on a pan. Instead, use the following procedure:

1 Determine the mass of an empty container, such as a beaker.

2 Pour the substance into the container, and measure the total mass of the substance and the container.

3 Subtract the mass of the empty container from the total mass to find the mass of the substance.

The Metric System and SI Units

Scientists use International System (SI) units for measurements of distance, volume, mass, and temperature. The International System is based on multiples of ten and the metric system of measurement.

Basic SI Units		
Property	Name	Symbol
length	meter	m
volume	liter	L
mass	kilogram	kg
temperature	kelvin	K

SI Prefixes		
Prefix	Symbol	Multiple of 10
kilo-	k	1000
hecto-	h	100
deca-	da	10
deci-	d	$0.1 \left(\frac{1}{10}\right)$
centi-	c	$0.01 \left(\frac{1}{100}\right)$
milli-	m	$0.001 \left(\frac{1}{1000}\right)$

Changing Metric Units

You can change from one unit to another in the metric system by multiplying or dividing by a power of 10.

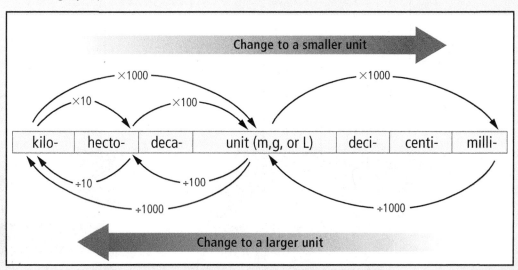

Example

Change 0.64 liters to milliliters.

(1) Decide whether to multiply or divide.

(2) Select the power of 10.

ANSWER 0.64 L = 640 mL

Change to a smaller unit by multiplying.

mL ◄── × 1000 ── L

0.64 × 1000 = **640.**

Example

Change 23.6 grams to kilograms.

(1) Decide whether to multiply or divide.

(2) Select the power of 10.

ANSWER 23.6 g = 0.0236 kg

Change to a larger unit by dividing.

g ── ÷ 1000 ──► kg

23.6 ÷ 1000 = **0.0236**

Temperature Conversions

Even though the kelvin is the SI base unit of temperature, the degree Celsius will be the unit you use most often in your science studies. The formulas below show the relationships between temperatures in degrees Fahrenheit (°F), degrees Celsius (°C), and kelvins (K).

$$°C = \frac{5}{9}(°F - 32)$$

$$°F = \frac{9}{5}°C + 32$$

$$K = °C + 273$$

See page R42 for help with using formulas.

Examples of Temperature Conversions

Condition	Degrees Celsius	Degrees Fahrenheit
Freezing point of water	0	32
Cool day	10	50
Mild day	20	68
Warm day	30	86
Normal body temperature	37	98.6
Very hot day	40	104
Boiling point of water	100	212

Converting Between SI and U.S. Customary Units

Use the chart below when you need to convert between SI units and U.S. customary units.

SI Unit	From SI to U.S. Customary			From U.S. Customary to SI		
Length	When you know	multiply by	to find	When you know	multiply by	to find
kilometer (km) = 1000 m	kilometers	0.62	miles	miles	1.61	kilometers
meter (m) = 100 cm	meters	3.28	feet	feet	0.3048	meters
centimeter (cm) = 10 mm	centimeters	0.39	inches	inches	2.54	centimeters
millimeter (mm) = 0.1 cm	millimeters	0.04	inches	inches	25.4	millimeters
Area	When you know	multiply by	to find	When you know	multiply by	to find
square kilometer (km^2)	square kilometers	0.39	square miles	square miles	2.59	square kilometers
square meter (m^2)	square meters	1.2	square yards	square yards	0.84	square meters
square centimeter (cm^2)	square centimeters	0.155	square inches	square inches	6.45	square centimeters
Volume	When you know	multiply by	to find	When you know	multiply by	to find
liter (L) = 1000 mL	liters	1.06	quarts	quarts	0.95	liters
	liters	0.26	gallons	gallons	3.79	liters
	liters	4.23	cups	cups	0.24	liters
	liters	2.12	pints	pints	0.47	liters
milliliter (mL) = 0.001 L	milliliters	0.20	teaspoons	teaspoons	4.93	milliliters
	milliliters	0.07	tablespoons	tablespoons	14.79	milliliters
	milliliters	0.03	fluid ounces	fluid ounces	29.57	milliliters
Mass	When you know	multiply by	to find	When you know	multiply by	to find
kilogram (kg) = 1000 g	kilograms	2.2	pounds	pounds	0.45	kilograms
gram (g) = 1000 mg	grams	0.035	ounces	ounces	28.35	grams

Precision and Accuracy

When you do an experiment, it is important that your methods, observations, and data be both precise and accurate.

low precision

precision, but not accuracy

precision and accuracy

Precision

In science, **precision** is the exactness and consistency of measurements. For example, measurements made with a ruler that has both centimeter and millimeter markings would be more precise than measurements made with a ruler that has only centimeter markings. Another indicator of precision is the care taken to make sure that methods and observations are as exact and consistent as possible. Every time a particular experiment is done, the same procedure should be used. Precision is necessary because experiments are repeated several times and if the procedure changes, the results will change.

EXAMPLE

Suppose you are measuring temperatures over a two-week period. Your precision will be greater if you measure each temperature at the same place, at the same time of day, and with the same thermometer than if you change any of these factors from one day to the next.

Accuracy

In science, it is possible to be precise but not accurate. **Accuracy** depends on the difference between a measurement and an actual value. The smaller the difference, the more accurate the measurement.

EXAMPLE

Suppose you look at a stream and estimate that it is about 1 meter wide at a particular place. You decide to check your estimate by measuring the stream with a meter stick, and you determine that the stream is 1.32 meters wide. However, because it is hard to measure the width of a stream with a meter stick, it turns out that you didn't do a very good job. The stream is actually 1.14 meters wide. Therefore, even though your estimate was less precise than your measurement, your estimate was actually more accurate.

Making Data Tables and Graphs

Data tables and graphs are useful tools for both recording and communicating scientific data.

Making Data Tables

You can use a **data table** to organize and record the measurements that you make. Some examples of information that might be recorded in data tables are frequencies, times, and amounts.

EXAMPLE

Suppose you are investigating photosynthesis in two elodea plants. One sits in direct sunlight, and the other sits in a dimly lit room. You measure the rate of photosynthesis by counting the number of bubbles in the jar every ten minutes.

1. Title and number your data table.
2. Decide how you will organize the table into columns and rows.
3. Any units, such as seconds or degrees, should be included in column headings, not in the individual cells.

Table 1. Number of Bubbles from Elodea

Time (min)	Sunlight	Dim Light
0	0	0
10	15	5
20	25	8
30	32	7
40	41	10
50	47	9
60	42	9

> Always number and title data tables.

The data in the table above could also be organized in a different way.

Table 1. Number of Bubbles from Elodea

Light Condition	Time (min)						
	0	10	20	30	40	50	60
Sunlight	0	15	25	32	41	47	42
Dim light	0	5	8	7	10	9	9

> Put units in column heading.

Making Line Graphs

You can use a **line graph** to show a relationship between variables. Line graphs are particularly useful for showing changes in variables over time.

EXAMPLE

Suppose you are interested in graphing temperature data that you collected over the course of a day.

Table 1. Outside Temperature During the Day on March 7

	Time of Day						
	7:00 A.M.	9:00 A.M.	11:00 A.M.	1:00 P.M.	3:00 P.M.	5:00 P.M.	7:00 P.M.
Temp (°C)	8	9	11	14	12	10	6

1. Use the vertical axis of your line graph for the variable that you are measuring—temperature.

2. Choose scales for both the horizontal axis and the vertical axis of the graph. You should have two points more than you need on the vertical axis, and the horizontal axis should be long enough for all of the data points to fit.

3. Draw and label each axis.

4. Graph each value. First find the appropriate point on the scale of the horizontal axis. Imagine a line that rises vertically from that place on the scale. Then find the corresponding value on the vertical axis, and imagine a line that moves horizontally from that value. The point where these two imaginary lines intersect is where the value should be plotted.

5. Connect the points with straight lines.

Be sure to add a number and a title to your graph.

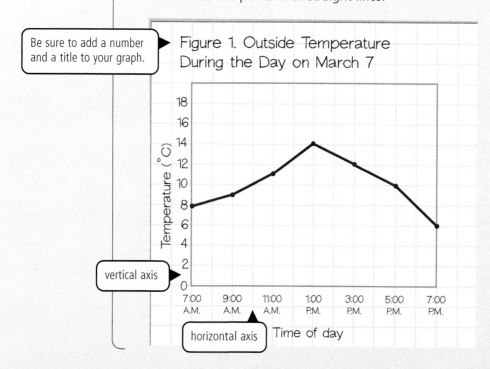

Figure 1. Outside Temperature During the Day on March 7

vertical axis

horizontal axis

Time of day

Making Circle Graphs

You can use a **circle graph,** sometimes called a pie chart, to represent data as parts of a circle. Circle graphs are used only when the data can be expressed as percentages of a whole. The entire circle shown in a circle graph is equal to 100 percent of the data.

EXAMPLE

Suppose you identified the species of each mature tree growing in a small wooded area. You organized your data in a table, but you also want to show the data in a circle graph.

1. To begin, find the total number of mature trees.

   $$56 + 34 + 22 + 10 + 28 = 150$$

2. To find the degree measure for each sector of the circle, write a fraction comparing the number of each tree species with the total number of trees. Then multiply the fraction by 360°.

   Oak: $\frac{56}{150} \times 360° = 134.4°$

3. Draw a circle. Use a protractor to draw the angle for each sector of the graph.

4. Color and label each sector of the graph.

5. Give the graph a number and title.

Table 1. Tree Species in Wooded Area

Species	Number of Specimens
Oak	56
Maple	34
Birch	22
Willow	10
Pine	28

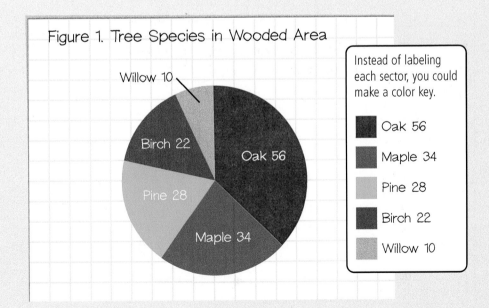

Figure 1. Tree Species in Wooded Area

Instead of labeling each sector, you could make a color key.

- Oak 56
- Maple 34
- Pine 28
- Birch 22
- Willow 10

Bar Graph

A **bar graph** is a type of graph in which the lengths of the bars are used to represent and compare data. A numerical scale is used to determine the lengths of the bars.

EXAMPLE

To determine the effect of water on seed sprouting, three cups were filled with sand, and ten seeds were planted in each. Different amounts of water were added to each cup over a three-day period.

Table 1. Effect of Water on Seed Sprouting

Daily Amount of Water (mL)	Number of Seeds That Sprouted After 3 Days in Sand
0	1
10	4
20	8

1. Choose a numerical scale. The greatest value is 8, so the end of the scale should have a value greater than 8, such as 10. Use equal increments along the scale, such as increments of 2.

2. Draw and label the axes. Mark intervals on the vertical axis according to the scale you chose.

3. Draw a bar for each data value. Use the scale to decide how long to make each bar.

Figure 1. Effect of Water on Seed Sprouting

Be sure to add a number and a title.

Label the scale.

Label each bar.

Double Bar Graph

A **double bar graph** is a bar graph that shows two sets of data. The two bars for each measurement are drawn next to each other.

EXAMPLE

The seed-sprouting experiment was done using both sand and potting soil. The data for sand and potting soil can be plotted on one graph.

1. Draw one set of bars, using the data for sand, as shown below.

2. Draw bars for the potting-soil data next to the bars for the sand data. Shade them a different color. Add a key.

Table 2. Effect of Water and Soil on Seed Sprouting

Daily Amount of Water (mL)	Number of Seeds That Sprouted After 3 Days in Sand	Number of Seeds That Sprouted After 3 Days in Potting Soil
0	1	2
10	4	5
20	8	9

Figure 2. Effect of Water and Soil on Seed Sprouting

Sand

Potting soil

Make a key to show what each color represents.

Leave room for "potting soil" bars.

Designing an Experiment

Use this section when designing or conducting an experiment.

Determining a Purpose

You can find a purpose for an experiment by doing research, by examining the results of a previous experiment, or by observing the world around you. An **experiment** is an organized procedure to study something under controlled conditions.

> Don't forget to learn as much as possible about your topic before you begin.

1. Write the purpose of your experiment as a question or problem that you want to investigate.

2. Write down research questions and begin searching for information that will help you design an experiment. Consult the library, the Internet, and other people as you conduct your research.

EXAMPLE

Middle school students observed an odor near the lake by their school. They also noticed that the water on the side of the lake near the school was greener than the water on the other side of the lake. The students did some research to learn more about their observations. They discovered that the odor and green color in the lake came from algae. They also discovered that a new fertilizer was being used on a field nearby. The students inferred that the use of the fertilizer might be related to the presence of the algae and designed a controlled experiment to find out whether they were right.

Problem

How does fertilizer affect the presence of algae in a lake?

Research Questions

- Have other experiments been done on this problem? If so, what did those experiments show?
- What kind of fertilizer is used on the field? How much?
- How do algae grow?
- How do people measure algae?
- Can fertilizer and algae be used safely in a lab? How?

> **Research**
> As you research, you may find a topic that is more interesting to you than your original topic, or learn that a procedure you wanted to use is not practical or safe. It is OK to change your purpose as you research.

Writing a Hypothesis

A **hypothesis** is a tentative explanation for an observation or scientific problem that can be tested by further investigation. You can write your hypothesis in the form of an "If . . . , then . . . , because . . ." statement.

Hypothesis

If the amount of fertilizer in lake water is increased, then the amount of algae will also increase, because fertilizers provide nutrients that algae need to grow.

Hypotheses
For help with hypotheses, refer to page R3.

Determining Materials

Make a list of all the materials you will need to do your experiment. Be specific, especially if someone else is helping you obtain the materials. Try to think of everything you will need.

Materials
- 1 large jar or container
- 4 identical smaller containers
- rubber gloves that also cover the arms
- sample of fertilizer-and-water solution
- eyedropper
- clear plastic wrap
- scissors
- masking tape
- marker
- ruler

Determining Variables and Constants

EXPERIMENTAL GROUP AND CONTROL GROUP

An experiment to determine how two factors are related always has two groups—a control group and an experimental group.

1. Design an experimental group. Include as many trials as possible in the experimental group in order to obtain reliable results.

2. Design a control group that is the same as the experimental group in every way possible, except for the factor you wish to test.

Experimental Group: two containers of lake water with one drop of fertilizer solution added to each

Control Group: two containers of lake water with no fertilizer solution added

Go back to your materials list and make sure you have enough items listed to cover both your experimental group and your control group.

VARIABLES AND CONSTANTS

Identify the variables and constants in your experiment. In a controlled experiment, a **variable** is any factor that can change. **Constants** are all of the factors that are the same in both the experimental group and the control group.

1. Read your hypothesis. The **independent variable** is the factor that you wish to test and that is manipulated or changed so that it can be tested. The independent variable is expressed in your hypothesis after the word *if*. Identify the independent variable in your laboratory report.

2. The **dependent variable** is the factor that you measure to gather results. It is expressed in your hypothesis after the word *then*. Identify the dependent variable in your laboratory report.

Hypothesis
If the amount of fertilizer in lake water is increased, then the amount of algae will also increase, because fertilizers provide nutrients that algae need to grow.

Table 1. Variables and Constants in Algae Experiment

Independent Variable	Dependent Variable	Constants
Amount of fertilizer in lake water	Amount of algae that grow	• Where the lake water is obtained • Type of container used • Light and temperature conditions where water will be stored

Set up your experiment so that you will test only one variable.

MEASURING THE DEPENDENT VARIABLE

Before starting your experiment, you need to define how you will measure the dependent variable. An **operational definition** is a description of the one particular way in which you will measure the dependent variable.

Your operational definition is important for several reasons. First, in any experiment there are several ways in which a dependent variable can be measured. Second, the procedure of the experiment depends on how you decide to measure the dependent variable. Third, your operational definition makes it possible for other people to evaluate and build on your experiment.

EXAMPLE 1

An operational definition of a dependent variable can be qualitative. That is, your measurement of the dependent variable can simply be an observation of whether a change occurs as a result of a change in the independent variable. This type of operational definition can be thought of as a "yes or no" measurement.

Table 2. Qualitative Operational Definition of Algae Growth

Independent Variable	Dependent Variable	Operational Definition
Amount of fertilizer in lake water	Amount of algae that grow	Algae grow in lake water

A qualitative measurement of a dependent variable is often easy to make and record. However, this type of information does not provide a great deal of detail in your experimental results.

EXAMPLE 2

An operational definition of a dependent variable can be quantitative. That is, your measurement of the dependent variable can be a number that shows how much change occurs as a result of a change in the independent variable.

Table 3. Quantitative Operational Definition of Algae Growth

Independent Variable	Dependent Variable	Operational Definition
Amount of fertilizer in lake water	Amount of algae that grow	Diameter of largest algal growth (in mm)

A quantitative measurement of a dependent variable can be more difficult to make and analyze than a qualitative measurement. However, this type of data provides much more information about your experiment and is often more useful.

Writing a Procedure

Write each step of your procedure. Start each step with a verb, or action word, and keep the steps short. Your procedure should be clear enough for someone else to use as instructions for repeating your experiment.

If necessary, go back to your materials list and add any materials that you left out.

Controlling Variables
The same amount of fertilizer solution must be added to two of the four containers.

Controlling Variables
All four containers must receive the same amount of light.

Procedure

1. Put on your gloves. Use the large container to obtain a sample of lake water.

2. Divide the sample of lake water equally among the four smaller containers.

3. Use the eyedropper to add one drop of fertilizer solution to two of the containers.

4. Use the masking tape and the marker to label the containers with your initials, the date, and the identifiers "Jar 1 with Fertilizer," "Jar 2 with Fertilizer," "Jar 1 without Fertilizer," and "Jar 2 without Fertilizer."

5. Cover the containers with clear plastic wrap. Use the scissors to punch ten holes in each of the covers.

6. Place all four containers on a window ledge. Make sure that they all receive the same amount of light.

7. Observe the containers every day for one week.

8. Use the ruler to measure the diameter of the largest clump of algae in each container, and record your measurements daily.

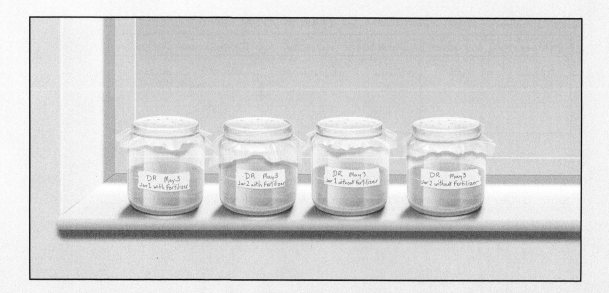

LAB HANDBOOK

Recording Observations

Once you have obtained all of your materials and your procedure has been approved, you can begin making experimental observations. Gather both quantitative and qualitative data. If something goes wrong during your procedure, make sure you record that too.

Observations
For help with making qualitative and quantitative observations, refer to page R2.

For more examples of data tables, see page R23.

Table 4. Fertilizer and Algae Growth

Date and Time	Experimental Group		Control Group		
	Jar 1 with Fertilizer (diameter of algae in mm)	Jar 2 with Fertilizer (diameter of algae in mm)	Jar 1 without Fertilizer (diameter of algae in mm)	Jar 2 without Fertilizer (diameter of algae in mm)	Observations
5/3 4:00 P.M.	0	0	0	0	condensation in all containers
5/4 4:00 P.M.	0	3	0	0	tiny green blobs in jar 2 with fertilizer
5/5 4:15 P.M.	4	5	0	3	green blobs in jars 1 and 2 with fertilizer and jar 2 without fertilizer
5/6 4:00 P.M.	5	6	0	4	water light green in jar 2 with fertilizer
5/7 4:00 P.M.	8	10	0	6	water light green in jars 1 and 2 with fertilizer and in jar 2 without fertilizer
5/8 3:30 P.M.	10	18	0	6	cover off jar 2 with fertilizer
5/9 3:30 P.M.	14	23	0	8	drew sketches of each container

Notice that on the sixth day, the observer found that the cover was off one of the containers. It is important to record observations of unintended factors because they might affect the results of the experiment.

Drawings of Samples Viewed Under Microscope on 5/9 at 100x

Use technology, such as a microscope, to help you make observations when possible.

| Jar 1 with Fertilizer | Jar 2 with Fertilizer | Jar 1 without Fertilizer | Jar 2 without Fertilizer |

Summarizing Results

To summarize your data, look at all of your observations together. Look for meaningful ways to present your observations. For example, you might average your data or make a graph to look for patterns. When possible, use spreadsheet software to help you analyze and present your data. The two graphs below show the same data.

EXAMPLE 1

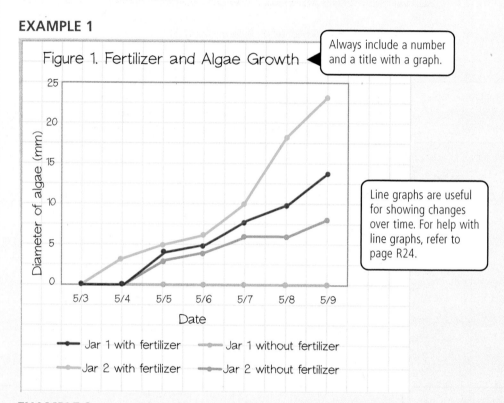

Always include a number and a title with a graph.

Line graphs are useful for showing changes over time. For help with line graphs, refer to page R24.

EXAMPLE 2

Bar graphs are useful for comparing different data sets. This bar graph has four bars for each day. Another way to present the data would be to calculate averages for the tests and the controls, and to show one test bar and one control bar for each day.

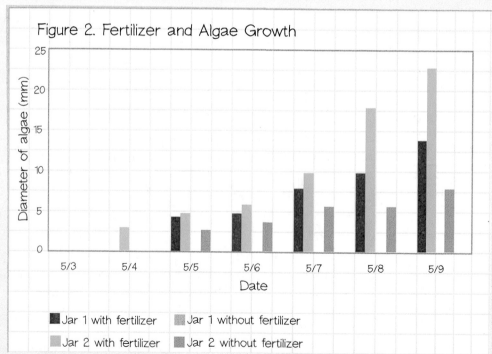

Drawing Conclusions

RESULTS AND INFERENCES

To draw conclusions from your experiment, first write your results. Then compare your results with your hypothesis. Do your results support your hypothesis? Be careful not to make inferences about factors that you did not test.

> For help with making inferences, see page R4.

Results and Inferences

The results of my experiment show that more algae grew in lake water to which fertilizer had been added than in lake water to which no fertilizer had been added. My hypothesis was supported. I infer that it is possible that the growth of algae in the lake was caused by the fertilizer used on the field.

> Notice that you cannot conclude from this experiment that the presence of algae in the lake was due only to the fertilizer.

QUESTIONS FOR FURTHER RESEARCH

Write a list of questions for further research and investigation. Your ideas may lead you to new experiments and discoveries.

Questions for Further Research

- What is the connection between the amount of fertilizer and algae growth?
- How do different brands of fertilizer affect algae growth?
- How would algae growth in the lake be affected if no fertilizer were used on the field?
- How do algae affect the lake and the other life in and around it?
- How does fertilizer affect the lake and the life in and around it?
- If fertilizer is getting into the lake, how is it getting there?

Math Handbook

Describing a Set of Data

Means, medians, modes, and ranges are important math tools for describing data sets such as the following widths of fossilized clamshells.

13 mm   25 mm   14 mm   21 mm   16 mm   23 mm   14 mm

Mean

The **mean** of a data set is the sum of the values divided by the number of values.

Example

To find the mean of the clamshell data, add the values and then divide the sum by the number of values.

$$\frac{13 \text{ mm} + 25 \text{ mm} + 14 \text{ mm} + 21 \text{ mm} + 16 \text{ mm} + 23 \text{ mm} + 14 \text{ mm}}{7} = \frac{126 \text{ mm}}{7} = 18 \text{ mm}$$

ANSWER The mean is 18 mm.

Median

The **median** of a data set is the middle value when the values are written in numerical order. If a data set has an even number of values, the median is the mean of the two middle values.

Example

To find the median of the clamshell data, arrange the values in order from least to greatest. The median is the middle value.

13 mm   14 mm   14 mm   16 mm   21 mm   23 mm   25 mm

ANSWER The median is 16 mm.

Mode

The **mode** of a data set is the value that occurs most often.

Example

To find the mode of the clamshell data, arrange the values in order from least to greatest and determine the value that occurs most often.

13 mm   14 mm   14 mm   16 mm   21 mm   23 mm   25 mm

ANSWER The mode is 14 mm.

A data set can have more than one mode or no mode. For example, the following data set has modes of 2 mm and 4 mm:

2 mm   2 mm   3 mm   4 mm   4 mm

The data set below has no mode, because no value occurs more often than any other.

2 mm   3 mm   4 mm   5 mm

Range

The **range** of a data set is the difference between the greatest value and the least value.

Example

To find the range of the clamshell data, arrange the values in order from least to greatest.

13 mm   14 mm   14 mm   16 mm   21 mm   23 mm   25 mm

Subtract the least value from the greatest value.

13 mm is the least value.
25 mm is the greatest value.

25 mm − 13 mm = 12 mm

ANSWER The range is 12 mm.

Using Ratios, Rates, and Proportions

You can use ratios and rates to compare values in data sets. You can use proportions to find unknown values.

Ratios

A **ratio** uses division to compare two values. The ratio of a value a to a nonzero value b can be written as $\frac{a}{b}$.

Example

The height of one plant is 8 centimeters. The height of another plant is 6 centimeters. To find the ratio of the height of the first plant to the height of the second plant, write a fraction and simplify it.

$$\frac{8 \text{ cm}}{6 \text{ cm}} = \frac{4 \times \overset{1}{\cancel{2}}}{3 \times \underset{1}{\cancel{2}}} = \frac{4}{3}$$

ANSWER The ratio of the plant heights is $\frac{4}{3}$.

You can also write the ratio $\frac{a}{b}$ as "a to b" or as $a:b$. For example, you can write the ratio of the plant heights as "4 to 3" or as $4:3$.

Rates

A **rate** is a ratio of two values expressed in different units. A unit rate is a rate with a denominator of 1 unit.

Example

A plant grew 6 centimeters in 2 days. The plant's rate of growth was $\frac{6 \text{ cm}}{2 \text{ days}}$. To describe the plant's growth in centimeters per day, write a unit rate.

Divide numerator and denominator by 2: $\frac{6 \text{ cm}}{2 \text{ days}} = \frac{6 \text{ cm} \div 2}{2 \text{ days} \div 2}$ You divide 2 days by 2 to get 1 day, so divide 6 cm by 2 also.

Simplify: $= \frac{3 \text{ cm}}{1 \text{ day}}$

ANSWER The plant's rate of growth is 3 centimeters per day.

Proportions

A **proportion** is an equation stating that two ratios are equivalent. To solve for an unknown value in a proportion, you can use cross products.

Example

If a plant grew 6 centimeters in 2 days, how many centimeters would it grow in 3 days (if its rate of growth is constant)?

$$\textit{Write a proportion:} \quad \frac{6\ cm}{2\ days} = \frac{x}{3\ days}$$

$$\textit{Set cross products:} \quad 6\ cm \cdot 3 = 2x$$

$$\textit{Multiply 6 and 3:} \quad 18\ cm = 2x$$

$$\textit{Divide each side by 2:} \quad \frac{18\ cm}{2} = \frac{2x}{2}$$

$$\textit{Simplify:} \quad 9\ cm = x$$

ANSWER The plant would grow 9 centimeters in 3 days.

Using Decimals, Fractions, and Percents

Decimals, fractions, and percentages are all ways of recording and representing data.

Decimals

A **decimal** is a number that is written in the base-ten place value system, in which a decimal point separates the ones and tenths digits. The values of each place is ten times that of the place to its right.

Example

A caterpillar traveled from point A to point C along the path shown.

A   36.9 cm   B   52.4 cm   C

ADDING DECIMALS To find the total distance traveled by the caterpillar, add the distance from A to B and the distance from B to C. Begin by lining up the decimal points. Then add the figures as you would whole numbers and bring down the decimal point.

$$\begin{array}{r} 36.9\ cm \\ +\ 52.4\ cm \\ \hline 89.3\ cm \end{array}$$

ANSWER The caterpillar traveled a total distance of 89.3 centimeters.

Example continued

SUBTRACTING DECIMALS To find how much farther the caterpillar traveled on the second leg of the journey, subtract the distance from *A* to *B* from the distance from *B* to *C*.

$$
\begin{array}{r}
52.4 \text{ cm} \\
- \ 36.9 \text{ cm} \\
\hline
15.5 \text{ cm}
\end{array}
$$

ANSWER The caterpillar traveled 15.5 centimeters farther on the second leg of the journey.

Example

A caterpillar is traveling from point *D* to point *F* along the path shown. The caterpillar travels at a speed of 9.6 centimeters per minute.

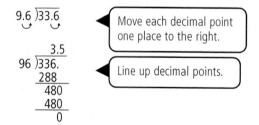

MULTIPLYING DECIMALS You can multiply decimals as you would whole numbers. The number of decimal places in the product is equal to the sum of the number of decimal places in the factors.

For instance, suppose it takes the caterpillar 1.5 minutes to go from *D* to *E*. To find the distance from *D* to *E*, multiply the caterpillar's speed by the time it took.

Align as shown.

$$
\begin{array}{rl}
9.6 & 1 \quad \text{decimal place} \\
\times \ 1.5 & + \ 1 \quad \text{decimal place} \\
\hline
480 & \\
96 & \\
\hline
14.40 & 2 \quad \text{decimal places}
\end{array}
$$

ANSWER The distance from *D* to *E* is 14.4 centimeters.

DIVIDING DECIMALS When you divide by a decimal, move the decimal points the same number of places in the divisor and the dividend to make the divisor a whole number.

For instance, to find the time it will take the caterpillar to travel from *E* to *F*, divide the distance from *E* to *F* by the caterpillar's speed.

$$
9.6\overline{)33.6}
$$
◀ Move each decimal point one place to the right.

$$
\begin{array}{r}
3.5 \\
96\overline{)336.} \\
\underline{288} \\
480 \\
\underline{480} \\
0
\end{array}
$$
◀ Line up decimal points.

ANSWER The caterpillar will travel from *E* to *F* in 3.5 minutes.

Fractions

A **fraction** is a number in the form $\frac{a}{b}$, where b is not equal to 0. A fraction is in **simplest form** if its numerator and denominator have a greatest common factor (GCF) of 1. To simplify a fraction, divide its numerator and denominator by their GCF.

Example

A caterpillar is 40 millimeters long. The head of the caterpillar is 6 millimeters long. To compare the length of the caterpillar's head with the caterpillar's total length, you can write and simplify a fraction that expresses the ratio of the two lengths.

Write the ratio of the two lengths: $\dfrac{\text{Length of head}}{\text{Total length}} = \dfrac{6 \text{ mm}}{40 \text{ mm}}$

Write numerator and denominator as products of numbers and the GCF: $= \dfrac{3 \times 2}{20 \times 2}$

Divide numerator and denominator by the GCF: $= \dfrac{3 \times \overset{1}{\cancel{2}}}{20 \times \underset{1}{\cancel{2}}}$

Simplify: $= \dfrac{3}{20}$

ANSWER In simplest form, the ratio of the lengths is $\frac{3}{20}$.

Percents

A **percent** is a ratio that compares a number to 100. The word *percent* means "per hundred" or "out of 100." The symbol for *percent* is %.

For instance, suppose 43 out of 100 caterpillars are female. You can represent this ratio as a percent, a decimal, or a fraction.

Percent	Decimal	Fraction
43%	0.43	$\frac{43}{100}$

Example

In the preceding example, the ratio of the length of the caterpillar's head to the caterpillar's total length is $\frac{3}{20}$. To write this ratio as a percent, write an equivalent fraction that has a denominator of 100.

Multiply numerator and denominator by 5: $\dfrac{3}{20} = \dfrac{3 \times 5}{20 \times 5}$

$= \dfrac{15}{100}$

Write as a percent: $= 15\%$

ANSWER The caterpillar's head represents 15 percent of its total length.

Using Formulas

A **formula** is an equation that shows the general relationship between two or more quantities.

In science, a formula often has a word form and a symbolic form. The formula below expresses Ohm's law.

The term *variable* is also used in science to refer to a factor that can change during an experiment.

Word Form

$$\text{Current} = \frac{\text{voltage}}{\text{resistance}}$$

Symbolic Form

$$I = \frac{V}{R}$$

In this formula, I, V, and R are variables. A mathematical **variable** is a symbol or letter that is used to represent one or more numbers.

Example

Suppose that you measure a voltage of 1.5 volts and a resistance of 15 ohms. You can use the formula for Ohm's law to find the current in amperes.

Write the formula for Ohm's law: $\quad I = \frac{V}{R}$

Substitute 1.5 volts for V and 15 ohms for R: $\quad I = \frac{1.5 \text{ volts}}{15 \text{ ohms}}$

Simplify: $\quad I = 0.1 \text{ amp}$

ANSWER The current is 0.1 ampere.

If you know the values of all variables but one in a formula, you can solve for the value of the unknown variable. For instance, Ohm's law can be used to find a voltage if you know the current and the resistance.

Example

Suppose that you know that a current is 0.2 amperes and the resistance is 18 ohms. Use the formula for Ohm's law to find the voltage in volts.

Write the formula for Ohm's law: $\qquad I = \frac{V}{R}$

Substitute 0.2 amp for I and 18 ohms for R: $\qquad 0.2 \text{ amp} = \frac{V}{18 \text{ ohms}}$

Multiply both sides by 18 ohms: $\quad 0.2 \text{ amp} \cdot 18 \text{ ohms} = V$

Simplify: $\qquad 3.6 \text{ volts} = V$

ANSWER The voltage is 3.6 volts.

Finding Areas

The area of a figure is the amount of surface the figure covers.

Area is measured in square units, such as square meters (m^2) or square centimeters (cm^2). Formulas for the areas of three common geometric figures are shown below.

Area = (side length)^2
$A = s^2$

Area = length × width
$A = lw$

Area = $\frac{1}{2}$ × base × height

$A = \frac{1}{2} bh$

Example

Each face of a halite crystal is a square like the one shown. You can find the area of the square by using the steps below.

3 mm

3 mm

Write the formula for the area of a square: $A = s^2$

Substitute 3 mm for s: $= (3 \text{ mm})^2$

Simplify: $= 9 \text{ mm}^2$

ANSWER The area of the square is 9 square millimeters.

Finding Volumes

The volume of a solid is the amount of space contained by the solid.

Volume is measured in cubic units, such as cubic meters (m^3) or cubic centimeters (cm^3). The volume of a rectangular prism is given by the formula shown below.

Volume = length × width × height
$V = lwh$

Example

A topaz crystal is a rectangular prism like the one shown. You can find the volume of the prism by using the steps below.

10 mm

12 mm

20 mm

Write the formula for the volume of a rectangular prism: $V = lwh$

Substitute dimensions: $= 20 \text{ mm} \times 12 \text{ mm} \times 10 \text{ mm}$

Simplify: $= 2400 \text{ mm}^3$

ANSWER The volume of the rectangular prism is 2400 cubic millimeters.

Using Significant Figures

The **significant figures** in a decimal are the digits that are warranted by the accuracy of a measuring device.

When you perform a calculation with measurements, the number of significant figures to include in the result depends in part on the number of significant figures in the measurements. When you multiply or divide measurements, your answer should have only as many significant figures as the measurement with the fewest significant figures.

Example

Using a balance and a graduated cylinder filled with water, you determined that a marble has a mass of 8.0 grams and a volume of 3.5 cubic centimeters. To calculate the density of the marble, divide the mass by the volume.

Write the formula for density: $\text{Density} = \dfrac{\text{mass}}{\text{Volume}}$

Substitute measurements: $= \dfrac{8.0 \text{ g}}{3.5 \text{ cm}^3}$

Use a calculator to divide: $\approx 2.285714286 \text{ g/cm}^3$

ANSWER Because the mass and the volume have two significant figures each, give the density to two significant figures. The marble has a density of 2.3 grams per cubic centimeter.

Using Scientific Notation

Scientific notation is a shorthand way to write very large or very small numbers. For example, 73,500,000,000,000,000,000,000 kg is the mass of the Moon. In scientific notation, it is 7.35×10^{22} kg.

Example

You can convert from standard form to scientific notation.

Standard Form	Scientific Notation
720,000	7.2×10^5
5 decimal places left	Exponent is 5.
0.000291	2.91×10^{-4}
4 decimal places right	Exponent is −4.

You can convert from scientific notation to standard form.

Scientific Notation	Standard Form
4.63×10^7	46,300,000
Exponent is 7.	7 decimal places right
1.08×10^{-6}	0.00000108
Exponent is −6.	6 decimal places left

Note-Taking Handbook

Note-Taking Strategies

Taking notes as you read helps you understand the information. The notes you take can also be used as a study guide for later review. This handbook presents several ways to organize your notes.

Content Frame

1. Make a chart in which each column represents a category.
2. Give each column a heading.
3. Write details under the headings.

NAME	GROUP	CHARACTERISTICS	DRAWING
snail	mollusks	mantle, shell	
ant	arthropods	six legs, exoskeleton	
earthworm	segmented worms	segmented body, circulatory and digestive systems	
heartworm	roundworms	digestive system	
sea star	echinoderms	spiny skin, tube feet	
jellyfish	cnidarians	stinging cells	

categories

details

Combination Notes

1. For each new idea or concept, write an informal outline of the information.
2. Make a sketch to illustrate the concept, and label it.

NOTES

Types of forces
- contact force
- gravity
- friction

forces on a box being pushed

contact force

gravity

friction

sketch with labels

informal outline

Make flash cards to help you study for a test. Write a concept on one side of each card and draw the sketch that goes with it on the other side. Use the cards to review concepts with a friend.

Main Idea and Detail Notes

1. In the left-hand column of a two-column chart, list main ideas. The blue headings express main ideas throughout this textbook.

2. In the right-hand column, write details that expand on each main idea.

You can shorten the headings in your chart. Be sure to use the most important words.

When studying for tests, cover up the detail notes column with a sheet of paper. Then use each main idea to form a question—such as "How does latitude affect climate?" Answer the question, and then uncover the detail notes column to check your answer.

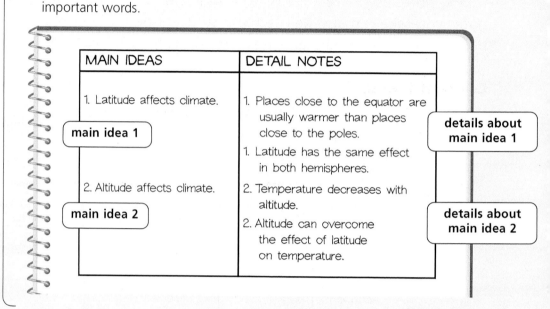

MAIN IDEAS	DETAIL NOTES
1. Latitude affects climate. **main idea 1**	1. Places close to the equator are usually warmer than places close to the poles. 1. Latitude has the same effect in both hemispheres. *details about main idea 1*
2. Altitude affects climate. **main idea 2**	2. Temperature decreases with altitude. 2. Altitude can overcome the effect of latitude on temperature. *details about main idea 2*

Main Idea Web

1. Write a main idea in a box.

2. Add boxes around it with related vocabulary terms and important details.

You can find definitions near highlighted terms.

definition of *work*
Work is the use of force to move an object.

formula
Work = force · distance

main idea
Force is necessary to do work.

The joule is the unit used to measure work.
definition of *joule*

Work depends on the size of a force.
important detail

Mind Map

1. Write a main idea in the center.

2. Add details that relate to one another and to the main idea.

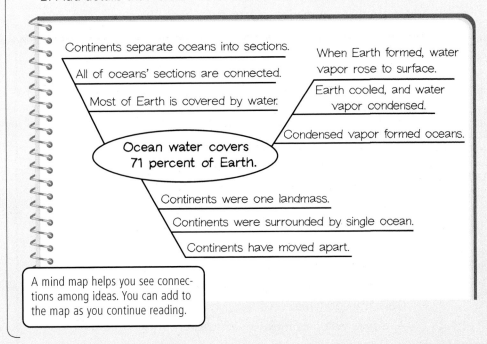

A mind map helps you see connections among ideas. You can add to the map as you continue reading.

Supporting Main Ideas

1. Write a main idea in a box.

2. Add boxes underneath with information—such as reasons, explanations, and examples—that supports the main idea.

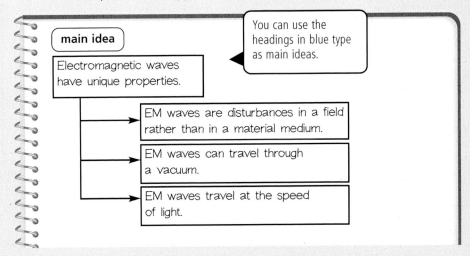

Outline

1. Copy the chapter title and headings from the book in the form of an outline.

2. Add notes that summarize in your own words what you read.

Cell Processes

I. Cells capture and release energy. ——— 1st key idea

   A. All cells need energy. ——— 1st subpoint of I

   B. Some cells capture light energy. ——— 2nd subpoint of I

1st detail about B ———   1. Process of photosynthesis

2nd detail about B ———   2. Chloroplasts (site of photosynthesis)

     3. Carbon dioxide and water as raw materials

     4. Glucose and oxygen as products

   C. All cells release energy.

     1. Process of cellular respiration

     2. Fermentation of sugar to carbon dioxide

     3. Bacteria that carry out fermentation

II. Cells transport materials through membranes.

   A. Some materials move by diffusion.

     1. Particle movement from higher to lower concentrations

     2. Movement of water through membrane (osmosis)

   B. Some transport requires energy.

     1. Active transport

     2. Examples of active transport

Correct Outline Form
Include a title.

Arrange key ideas, subpoints, and details as shown.

Indent the divisions of the outline as shown.

Use the same grammatical form for items of the same rank. For example, if A is a sentence, B must also be a sentence.

You must have at least two main ideas or subpoints. That is, every A must be followed by a B, and every 1 must be followed by a 2.

Concept Map

1. Write an important concept in a large oval.
2. Add details related to the concept in smaller ovals.
3. Write linking words on arrows that connect the ovals.

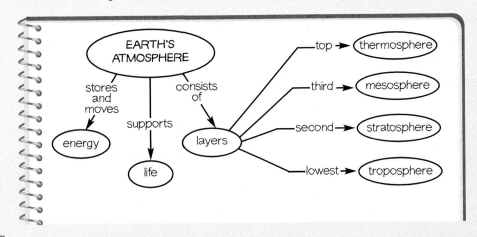

The main ideas or concepts can often be found in the blue headings. An example is "The atmosphere stores and moves energy." Use nouns from these concepts in the ovals, and use the verb or verbs on the lines.

Venn Diagram

1. Draw two overlapping circles, one for each item that you are comparing.
2. In the overlapping section, list the characteristics that are shared by both items.
3. In the outer sections, list the characteristics that are peculiar to each item.
4. Write a summary that describes the information in the Venn diagram.

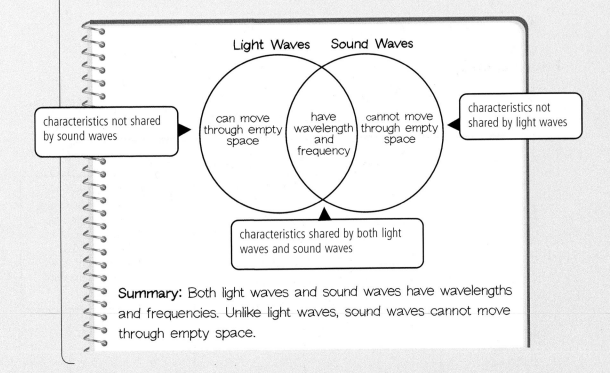

Summary: Both light waves and sound waves have wavelengths and frequencies. Unlike light waves, sound waves cannot move through empty space.

Vocabulary Strategies

Important terms are highlighted in this book. A definition of each term can be found in the sentence or paragraph where the term appears. You can also find definitions in the Glossary. Taking notes about vocabulary terms helps you understand and remember what you read.

Description Wheel

1. Write a term inside a circle.
2. Write words that describe the term on "spokes" attached to the circle.

When studying for a test with a friend, read the phrases on the spokes one at a time until your friend identifies the correct term.

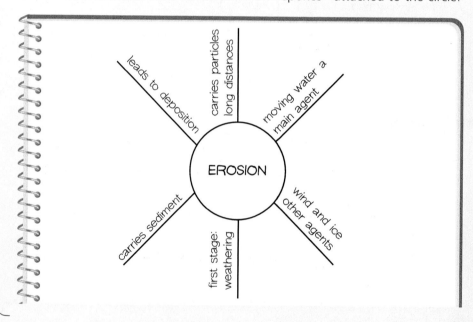

Four Square

1. Write a term in the center.
2. Write details in the four areas around the term.

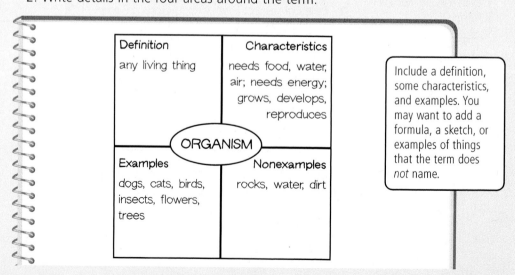

Include a definition, some characteristics, and examples. You may want to add a formula, a sketch, or examples of things that the term does *not* name.

NOTE-TAKING HANDBOOK

Frame Game

1. Write a term in the center.
2. Frame the term with details.

> Include examples, descriptions, sketches, or sentences that use the term in context. Change the frame to fit each new term.

Magnet Word

1. Write a term on the magnet.
2. On the lines, add details related to the term.

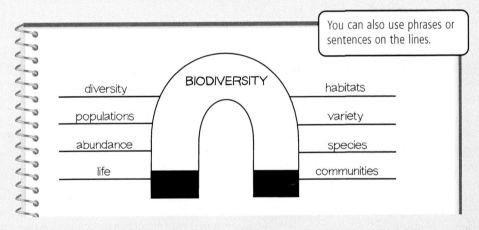

> You can also use phrases or sentences on the lines.

Word Triangle

1. Write a term and its definition in the bottom section.
2. In the middle section, write a sentence in which the term is used correctly.
3. In the top section, draw a small picture to illustrate the term.

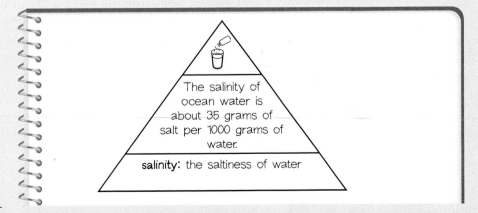

Glossary

GLOSSARY

A

alternating current AC
Electric current that reverses direction at regular intervals. (p. 97)

corriente alterna Corriente eléctrica que invierte su dirección a intervalos regulares.

ampere amp
The unit of measurement of electric current, which is equal to one coulomb per second. The number of amps flowing through a circuit equals the circuit's amperage. (p. 29)

amperio La unidad de medición de la corriente eléctrica, la cual es igual a un culombio por segundo. El número de amperios fluyendo por un circuito es igual al amperaje del circuito.

analog
Represented by a continuous but varying quantity, such as a wave. In electronics, analog information is represented by a continuous but varying electrical signal. (p. 60)

análogo Que es representado por una cantidad variante pero continua, como una onda. En la electrónica, la información análoga se representa mediante una señal eléctrica continua pero variante.

atom
The smallest particle of an element that has the chemical properties of that element. (p. xv)

átomo La partícula más pequeña de un elemento que tiene las propiedades químicas de ese elemento.

B

binary code
A coding system in which information is represented by two figures, such as 1 and 0. (p. 58)

código binario Un sistema de codificación en el cual la información se representa con dos números, como el 1 y el 0.

C

circuit
A closed path through which charge can flow. (p. 43)

circuito Una trayectoria cerrada por la cual puede fluir una carga.

compound
A substance made up of two or more different types of atoms bonded together.

compuesto Una sustancia formada por dos o más diferentes tipos de átomos enlazados.

computer
An electronic device that processes digital information. (p. 61)

computadora Un aparato electrónico que procesa información digital.

conductor
1. A material that transfers electric charge easily (p. 22).
2. A material that transfers energy easily.
conductor 1. Un material que transfiere cargas eléctricas fácilmente. 2. Un material que transfiere energía fácilmente.

cycle
n. A series of events or actions that repeat themselves regularly; a physical and/or chemical process in which one material continually changes locations and/or forms. Examples include the water cycle, the carbon cycle, and the rock cycle.

v. To move through a repeating series of events or actions.

ciclo *s.* Una serie de eventos o acciones que se repiten regularmente; un proceso físico y/o químico en el cual un material cambia continuamente de lugar y/o forma. Ejemplos: el ciclo del agua, el ciclo del carbono y el ciclo de las rocas.

D

data
Information gathered by observation or experimentation that can be used in calculating or reasoning. *Data* is a plural word; the singular is datum.

datos Información reunida mediante observación o experimentación y que se puede usar para calcular o para razonar.

density
A property of matter representing the mass per unit volume.

densidad Una propiedad de la materia que representa la masa por unidad de volumen.

digital
Represented by numbers. In electronics, digital information is represented by the numbers 1 and 0, signaled by a circuit that is either on or off. (p. 58)

digital Que es representado por números. En la electrónica, la información digital es representada por los números 1 y 0, señalados por un circuito que está encendido o apagado.

direct current DC
Electric current that flows in one direction only. (p. 97)

corriente directa Corriente eléctrica que fluye en una sola dirección.

E

electric cell
A device that produces electric current using the chemical or physical properties of different materials. A battery consists of two or more cells linked together. (p. 31)

celda eléctrica Un aparato que produce corriente eléctrica usando las propiedades químicas o físicas de diferentes materiales. Una pila consiste de dos o más celdas conectadas.

electric charge
A property that allows one object to exert an electric force on another object without touching it. Electric charge can be positive or negative: positive charge is a property of the proton, while negative charge is a property of the electron. (p. 10)

carga eléctrica Una propiedad que permite a un objeto ejercer una fuerza eléctrica sobre otro objeto sin tocarlo. La carga eléctrica puede ser positiva o negativa: la carga positiva es una propiedad del protón mientras que la carga negativa es una propiedad del electrón.

electric current
A continuous flow of electric charge, which is measured in amperes. (p. 28)

corriente eléctrica Un flujo continuo de una carga eléctrica, el cual se mide en amperios.

electric field
An area surrounding a charged object, within which the object can exert an electric force on another object without touching it. (p. 10)

campo eléctrico Un área que rodea un objeto con carga, dentro del cual el objeto puede ejercer una fuerza eléctrica sobre otro objeto sin tocarlo.

electric potential
The amount of potential energy per unit charge that a static charge or electric current has. Electric potential is measured in volts and is often called voltage. (p. 19)

potencial eléctrico La cantidad de energía potencial por unidad de carga que tiene una carga estática o una corriente eléctrica. El potencial eléctrico se mide en voltios y a menudo se llama voltaje.

electric power
The rate at which electrical energy is generated from, or converted into, another source of energy, such as kinetic energy. (p. 102)

potencia eléctrica El ritmo al cual se genera energía eléctrica a partir de, o se convierte en, otra fuente de energía, como energía cinética.

electromagnet
A magnet that consists of a piece of iron or steel inside a coil of current-carrying wire. (p. 90)

electroimán Un imán que consiste de un pedazo de hierro o de acero dentro de una bobina de alambre por la cual fluye una corriente eléctrica.

electromagnetism
Magnetism that results from the flow of electric charge. (p. 89)

electromagnetismo Magnetismo que resulta del flujo de una carga eléctrica.

electron
A negatively charged particle located outside an atom's nucleus.

electrón Una partícula con cargada negativamente localizada fuera del núcleo de un átomo.

electronic

adj. Operating by means of an electrical signal. An electronic device is a device that uses electric current to represent coded information. (p. 57)

n. An electronic device or system, such as a computer, calculator, CD player, or game system.

electrónico *adj.* Que opera por medio de una señal eléctrica. Un aparato electrónico es un aparato que usa corriente eléctrica para representar información codificada.

element

A substance that cannot be broken down into a simpler substance by ordinary chemical changes. An element consists of atoms of only one type. (p. xv)

elemento Una sustancia que no puede descomponerse en otra sustancia más simple por medio de cambios químicos normales. Un elemento consta de átomos de un solo tipo.

energy

The ability to do work or to cause a change. For example, the energy of a moving bowling ball knocks over pins; energy from food allows animals to move and to grow; and energy from the Sun heats Earth's surface and atmosphere, which causes air to move. (p. xix)

energía La capacidad para trabajar o causar un cambio. Por ejemplo, la energía de una bola de boliche en movimiento tumba los pinos; la energía proveniente de su alimento permite a los animales moverse y crecer; la energía del Sol calienta la superficie y la atmósfera de la Tierra, lo que ocasiona que el aire se mueva.

experiment

An organized procedure to study something under controlled conditions. (p. xxiv)

experimento Un procedimiento organizado para estudiar algo bajo condiciones controladas.

F

force

A push or a pull; something that changes the motion of an object. (p. xxi)

fuerza Un empuje o un jalón; algo que cambia el movimiento de un objeto.

friction

A force that resists the motion between two surfaces in contact. (p. xxi)

fricción Una fuerza que resiste el movimiento entre dos superficies en contacto.

G

generator

A device that converts kinetic energy, or the energy of motion, into electrical energy. Generators produce electric current by rotating a magnet within a coil of wire or rotating a coil of wire within a magnetic field. (p. 96)

generador Un aparato que convierte energía cinética, o la energía del movimiento, a energía eléctrica. Los generadores producen corriente eléctrica al girar un imán dentro de una bobina de alambre o haciendo rotar una bobina de alambre dentro de un campo magnético.

gravity

The force that objects exert on each other because of their mass. (p. xxi)

gravedad La fuerza que los objetos ejercen entre sí debido a su masa.

grounding

The creation of a harmless, low-resistance path—a ground—for electricity to follow. Grounding is an important electrical safety procedure. (p. 25)

conexión a tierra La creación de una trayectoria inofensiva, de baja resistencia—una tierra—para que la siga la electricidad. La conexión a tierra es un importante procedimiento de seguridad eléctrica.

H

hypothesis

A tentative explanation for an observation or phenomenon. A hypothesis is used to make testable predictions. (p. xxiv)

hipótesis Una explicación provisional de una observación o de un fenómeno. Una hipótesis se usa para hacer predicciones que se pueden probar.

I

induction

The build-up of a static charge in an object when the object is close to, but not touching, a charged object. (p. 13)

inducción La acumulación de carga estática en un objeto cuando el objeto está cercano a, pero no en contacto con, un objeto con carga.

insulator
1. A material that does not transfer electric charge easily. (p. 22) 2. A material that does not transfer energy easily.

aislante 1. Un material que no transfiere cargas eléctricas fácilmente. 2. Un material que no transfiere energía fácilmente.

J, K

joule (jool) J
A unit used to measure energy and work. One calorie is equal to 4.18 joules of energy; one joule of work is done when a force of one newton moves an object one meter.

julio Una unidad que se usa para medir la energía y el trabajo. Una caloría es igual a 4.18 julios de energía; se hace un joule de trabajo cuando una fuerza de un newton mueve un objeto un metro.

kilowatt kW
A unit of measurement for power equal to 1000 watts. (p. 104)

kilovatio Una unidad de medición para la potencia equivalente a 1000 vatios.

kilowatt-hour kWh
The unit of measurement for electrical energy equal to one kilowatt of power over a one-hour period. (p. 105)

kilovatio-hora La unidad de medición de energía eléctrica igual a un kilovatio de potencia en un período de una hora.

L

law
In science, a rule or principle describing a physical relationship that always works in the same way under the same conditions. The law of conservation of energy is an example.

ley En las ciencias, una regla o un principio que describe una relación física que siempre funciona de la misma manera bajo las mismas condiciones. La ley de la conservación de la energía es un ejemplo.

law of conservation of energy
A law stating that no matter how energy is transferred or transformed, it continues to exist in one form or another. (p. xix)

ley de la conservación de la energía Una ley que establece que no importa cómo se transfiere o transforma la energía, toda la energía sigue presente en alguna forma u otra.

M, N

magnet
An object that attracts certain other materials, particularly iron and steel. (p. 79)

imán Un objeto que atrae a ciertos otros materiales, especialmente al hierro y al acero.

magnetic domain
A group of atoms whose magnetic fields align, or point in the same direction. Magnetic materials have magnetic domains, whereas nonmagnetic materials do not. (p. 83)

dominio magnético Un grupo de átomos cuyos campos magnéticos se alinean, o apuntan en la misma dirección. Los materiales magnéticos tienen dominios magnéticos mientras que los materiales no magnéticos no tienen.

magnetic field
An area surrounding a magnet within which the magnet can exert a force. Magnetic fields are concentrated into a pattern of lines that extend from the magnet's north pole to its south pole. (p. 81)

campo magnético Un área alrededor de un imán dentro del cual el imán puede ejercer una fuerza. Los campos magnéticos se concentran en un patrón de líneas que se extienden del polo norte del imán a su polo sur.

magnetic pole
One of two ends of a magnet where the magnetic force is the strongest. Every magnet has two poles.

polo magnético Uno de dos extremos de un imán donde la fuerza magnética es lo más fuerte. Todos los imanes tienen dos polos.

magnetism
The force exerted by a magnet. Opposite poles of two magnets attract, or pull together, whereas like poles of two magnets repel, or push apart. (p. 80)

magnetismo La fuerza que ejerce un imán. Los polos opuestos de dos imanes se atraen, o jalan hacia si, mientras que los polos iguales de dos imanes se repelen, o se empujan para alejarse uno del otro.

mass
A measure of how much matter an object is made of. (p. xv)

masa Una medida de la cantidad de materia de la que está compuesto un objeto.

matter

Anything that has mass and volume. Matter exists ordinarily as a solid, a liquid, or a gas. (p. xv)

materia Todo lo que tiene masa y volumen. Generalmente la materia existe como sólido, líquido o gas.

molecule

A group of atoms that are held together by covalent bonds so that they move as a single unit. (p. xv)

molécula Un grupo de átomos que están unidos mediante enlaces covalentes de tal manera que se mueven como una sola unidad.

O

ohm Ω

The unit of measurement for electrical resistance. (p. 23)

ohmio La unidad de medición para la resistencia eléctrica.

Ohm's law

The mathematical relationship among current, voltage, and resistance, expressed in the formula $I = V/R$ (current = voltage/resistance). (p. 29)

ley de Ohm La relación matemática entre la corriente, el voltaje y la resistencia, expresada en la fórmula $I = V/R$ (corriente = voltaje/resistencia).

P, Q

parallel circuit

A circuit in which current follows more than one path. Each device that is wired in a parallel circuit has its own path to and from the voltage source. (p. 53)

circuito paralelo Un circuito en el cual la corriente sigue más de una trayectoria. Cada aparato que está conectado a un circuito paralelo tiene su propia trayectoria desde y hacia la fuente de voltaje.

proton

A positively charged particle located in an atom's nucleus.

protón Una partícula con carga positiva localizada en el núcleo de un átomo.

R

resistance

The property of a material that determines how easily a charge can move through it. Resistance is measured in ohms. (p. 29)

resistencia La propiedad de un material que determina qué tan fácilmente puede moverse una carga a través de él. La resistencia se mide en ohmios.

resistor

An electrical device that slows the flow of charge in a circuit. (p. 44)

resistencia Un aparato eléctrico que hace más lento el flujo de carga en un circuito.

S

series circuit

A circuit in which current follows a single path. Each device that is wired in a series circuit shares a path to and from the voltage source. (p. 52)

circuito en serie Un circuito en el cual la corriente sigue una sola trayectoria. Cada aparato conectado a un circuito en serie comparte una trayectoria desde y hacia la fuente de voltaje.

short circuit

An unintended and undesired path connecting one part of a circuit with another. (p. 46)

corto circuito Una trayectoria no intencionada y no deseada que conecta una parte de un circuito con otra.

static charge

The buildup of electric charge in an object caused by the uneven distribution of charged particles. (p. 11)

carga estática La acumulación de carga eléctrica en un objeto ocasionada por la desigual distribución de partículas con carga.

system

A group of objects or phenomena that interact. A system can be as simple as a rope, a pulley, and a mass. It also can be as complex as the interaction of energy and matter in the four spheres of the Earth system.

sistema Un grupo de objetos o fenómenos que interactúan. Un sistema puede ser algo tan sencillo como una cuerda, una polea y una masa. También puede ser algo tan complejo como la interacción de la energía y la materia en las cuatro esferas del sistema de la Tierra.

T, U

technology

The use of scientific knowledge to solve problems or engineer new products, tools, or processes.

tecnología El uso de conocimientos científicos para resolver problemas o para diseñar nuevos productos, herramientas o procesos.

theory

In science, a set of widely accepted explanations of observations and phenomena. A theory is a well-tested explanation that is consistent with all available evidence.

teoría En las ciencias, un conjunto de explicaciones de observaciones y fenómenos que es ampliamente aceptado. Una teoría es una explicación bien probada que es consecuente con la evidencia disponible.

transformer

A device that uses electromagnetism to increase or decrease voltage. A transformer is often used in the distribution of current from power plants. (p. 99)

transformador Un aparato que usa electromagnetismo para aumentar o disminuir el voltaje. A menudo se usa un transformador en la distribución de corriente desde las centrales eléctricas.

V

variable

Any factor that can change in a controlled experiment, observation, or model. (p. R30)

variable Cualquier factor que puede cambiar en un experimento controlado, en una observación o en un modelo.

volt V

The unit of measurement for electric potential, which is equal to one joule per coulomb. The number of volts of an electric charge equals the charge's voltage. (p. 19)

voltio La unidad de medición para el potencial eléctrico, el cual es igual a un julio por segundo por culombio. El número de voltios de una carga eléctrica es igual al voltaje de la carga.

volume

An amount of three-dimensional space, often used to describe the space that an object takes up. (p. xv)

volumen Una cantidad de espacio tridimensional; a menudo se usa este término para describir el espacio que ocupa un objeto.

W, X, Y, Z

watt W

The unit of measurement for power, which is equal to one joule of work done or energy transferred in one second. For example, a 75 W light bulb converts electrical energy into heat and light at a rate of 75 joules per second. (p. 104)

vatio La unidad de medición de la potencia, el cual es igual a un julio de trabajo realizado o energía transferida en un segundo. Por ejemplo, una bombilla de 75 W convierte energía eléctrica a calor y luz a un ritmo de 75 julios por segundo.

Index

Page numbers for definitions are printed in **boldface** type.
Page numbers for illustrations, maps, and charts are printed in *italics*.

M

maglev train, 80, *80*
magnetic domain, **82,** 83
magnetic field, **81,** *81*, 89, *89*, 108
    of Earth, *84*, 84–85
magnetic force. *See* magnetism
magnetic north pole, 85
magnetic poles, **80,** *80*, 108
magnetism, xxi, **80,** 108
    atmosphere and, 86
    control of voltage, 99
    electricity and, 88
    electromagnetism, *89*, **89**
    magnetic materials, 82, *82*, 83
    production of electric current, 95, 108
magnets, *xxiii*, **79,** 82, 108
    Earth, *84*, 84–85
    healing properties of, 87
    permanent, 84
    temporary, 84
    vs. other materials, *83*
mass, **xv**
math skills
    area, **R43**
    decimal, **R39,** R40
    describing a set of data, R36–R37
    examples, 35, 56, 107
    formulas, 29, 104, 105, 107, **R42**
    fractions, **R41**
    mean, **R36**
    median, **R36**
    mode, **R37**
    percents, 56, **R41**
    proportions, **R39**
    range, **R37**
    rates, **R38**
    ratios, **R38**
    scientific notation, **R44**
    significant figures, 107, **R44**
    variables, 35
    volume, **R43**
matter, xiv–xvii, **xv**
    conservation of, xvii
    electrical charge property, 9, 36
    forms of, xvi–xvii
    movement of, xvii
    particles and, xiv–xv
    physical forces and, xx
mean, **R36**
median, **R36**
metric system, R20–R21
    changing metric units, R20, *R20*
    converting between US. customary units, R21, *R21*
    temperature conversion, R21, *R21*

microchip, 61
microscope, *R14,* R14–R15
    making a slide or wet mount, R15, *R15*
    scanning tunneling (STM), *xxiv*
    viewing an object, R15
MIDI, 5
mode, **R37**
molecule, **xv**
mosaic, *xiv*
motors, *92*, 92–94, *93*, 108
    electromagnets and, 92
    how they work, 92, *93*
    uses of, 94
multimeter, 30, *30*
music, electronics and, 2–5

N

Neptune, xxiv
net charge, 11
network, computer, 64
north pole, 81, 85
Northern Lights, 86, *86*
note-taking strategies, **R45–R49**
    combination notes, 8, *8*, R45, *R45*
    concept map, R49, *R49*
    content frame, R45, *R45*
    main idea and detail notes, R46, *R46*
    main idea web, 78, *78*, R46, *R46*
    mind map, R47, *R47*
    outline, 42, *42*, R48, *R48*
    supporting main ideas, R47, *R47*
    Venn diagram, R49, *R49*

O

observations, **xxiv, R2,** R5, R33
    qualitative, R2
    quantitative, R2
ohmmeter, 30
ohms, **23,** 29
Ohm's law, **29,** 29–30, 35, 36
open circuit, 45, *45*
operational definition, **R31**
opinion, **R9**
    different from fact, R9
output, 63, *63*
oxygen, fuel cells and, xxvii

P, Q

R

S

T

INDEX

Acknowledgments

Photography

Cover © Nick Koudis/Getty Images; **i** © Nick Koudis/Getty Images; **iii** *left (top to bottom)* Photograph of James Trefil by Evan Cantwell; Photograph of Rita Ann Calvo by Joseph Calvo; Photograph of Linda Carnine by Amilcar Cifuentes; Photograph of Sam Miller by Samuel Miller; *right (top to bottom)* Photograph of Kenneth Cutler by Kenneth A. Cutler; Photograph of Donald Steely by Marni Stamm; Photograph of Vicky Vachon by Redfern Photographics; **vi** © 2003 Barbara Ries; **vii** © Philip & Karen Smith/age fotostock america, inc.; **ix** Photographs by Sharon Hoogstraten; **xiv–xv** © Larry Hamill/age fotostock america, inc.; **xvi–xvii** © Fritz Poelking/age fotostock america, inc.; **xviii–xix** © Galen Rowell/Corbis; **xx–xxi** © Jack Affleck/SuperStock; **xxii** AP/Wide World Photos; **xxiii** © David Parker/IMI/University of Birmingham High, TC Consortium/Photo Researchers; **xxiv** *left* AP/Wide World Photos; *right Washington University Record;* **xxv** *top* © Kim Steele/Getty Images; *bottom* Reprinted with permission from S. Zhou et al., *SCIENCE* 291:1944–47. Copyright 2001 AAAS; **xxvi–xxvii** © Mike Fiala/Getty Images; **xxvii** *left* © Derek Trask/Corbis; *right* AP/Wide World Photos; **xxxii** © The Chedd-Angier Production Company; **2–3** © PHISH 2003; **3** © Jacques M. Chenet/Corbis; **4** *top* © John Foxx/ImageState; *bottom* © The Chedd-Angier Production Company; **5** © Stuart Hughes/Corbis; **6–7** AP/Wide World Photos; **7, 9** Photographs by Sharon Hoogstraten; **10** © Roger Ressmeyer/Corbis; **12** © Charles D. Winters/Photo Researchers; **14** Photograph by Sharon Hoogstraten; **16** © Maximilian Stock Ltd./Photo Researchers; **17** *left* © Ann and Rob Simpson; *right* © Patrice Ceisel/Visuals Unlimited; **18** Photograph by Sharon Hoogstraten; **19** © Steve Crise/Corbis; **21** © A & J Verkaik/Corbis; **22** Photograph by Sharon Hoogstraten; **23** *top* © Tim Wright/Corbis; *bottom* © Leland Bobb/Corbis; **24** © James D. Hooker/*Lighting Equipment News (UK)*; **26** *top left* © Scott T. Smith; All other photographs by Sharon Hoogstraten; **27, 28, 30, 31** Photographs by Sharon Hoogstraten; **33** © Chip Simons 2003; **34** Photo Courtesy of NASA/Getty Images; **35** © Julian Hirshowitz/Corbis; **36** © James D. Hooker/*Lighting Equipment News (UK)*; **40–41** © 2003 Barbara Ries; **41, 43** Photographs by Sharon Hoogstraten; **48** *left* © 1989 Paul Silverman/Fundamental Photographs, NYC; *right* Photograph by Sharon Hoogstraten; **49** © Creative Publishing International, Inc.; **50** *top left* © Gary Rhijnsburger/Masterfile; *center left* © Creative Publishing International, Inc.; **51, 52, 53, 54** Photographs by Sharon Hoogstraten; **56** © Robert Essel NYC/Corbis; **57** Photograph by Sharon Hoogstraten; **59** *top* AP/Wide World Photos; *bottom* Photograph by Sharon Hoogstraten; **61** © Kurt Stier/Corbis; **62, 63** © Gen Nishino/Getty Images; **64** © Donna Cox and Robert Patterson/ National Center for Supercomputing Applications, University of Illinois, Urbana; **65** AP/Wide World Photos; **66** *top* © Sheila Terry/Photo Researchers; *bottom* Photograph by Sharon Hoogstraten; **72** *top* © SPL/Photo Researchers; *bottom* The Granger Collection, New York; **73** *top left* © Philadelphia Museum of Art/Corbis; *top right* © Archivo Iconografico, S.A./Corbis; *bottom* © Adam Hart-Davis/ Photo Researchers; **74** *top* Science Museum/Science & Society Picture Library; *center left* © Bettmann/ Corbis; *center right* © Tony Craddock/Photo Researchers; *bottom* © Bettmann/Corbis; **75** *top left* © Alfred Pasieka/Photo Researchers; *top right* Photograph courtesy of Queens Borough Public Library, Long Island Division, Latimer Family Papers; *bottom* AP/Wide World Photos; **76–77** © Philip & Karen Smith/age fotostock america, inc.; **77, 79** Photographs by Sharon Hoogstraten; **80** *top* © Michael S. Yamashita/ Corbis; *bottom* Photograph by Sharon Hoogstraten; **81** Photographs by Sharon Hoogstraten; **82** © The Natural History Museum, London; **83** Photograph by Sharon Hoogstraten; **84** NASA; **85** Photograph by Sharon Hoogstraten; **86** © Chris Madeley/Photo Researchers; **87** © Brian Bahr/Getty Images; *inset* Courtesy of Discover Magnetics; **88, 90** Photographs by Sharon Hoogstraten; **91** *top* © George Haling/Photo Researchers; *bottom* © Dick Luria/Photo Researchers; **93** © G. K. & Vikki Hart/Getty Images; **95** Photograph by Sharon Hoogstraten; **97** © Ondrea Barbe/ Corbis; **98** Photograph by Sharon Hoogstraten; **99** © Randy M. Ury/Corbis; **100** *top* © Christopher Gould/Getty Images; *bottom* Photographs by Sharon Hoogstraten; **101** Photographs by Sharon Hoogstraten; **102** Bureau of Reclamation; **104** Courtesy of General Electric; **105** *top* Photograph by Sharon Hoogstraten; *bottom* © Maya Barnes/The Image Works; **107** © Mark Richards/PhotoEdit; **108** *top* Photograph by Sharon Hoogstraten; **R28** © Photodisc/Getty Images.

Illustrations

Ampersand Design Group **50**
Steve Cowden **60, 62–63, 68**
Stephen Durke **11, 12, 13, 21, 25, 31, 36, 39, 44, 46, 53, 68, 103, 108, 110**
Dan Stukenschneider **15, 33, 47, 49, 55, 92, 93, 94, 96, 97, 108, R11–R19, R22, R32**